DEBORAH BERKE

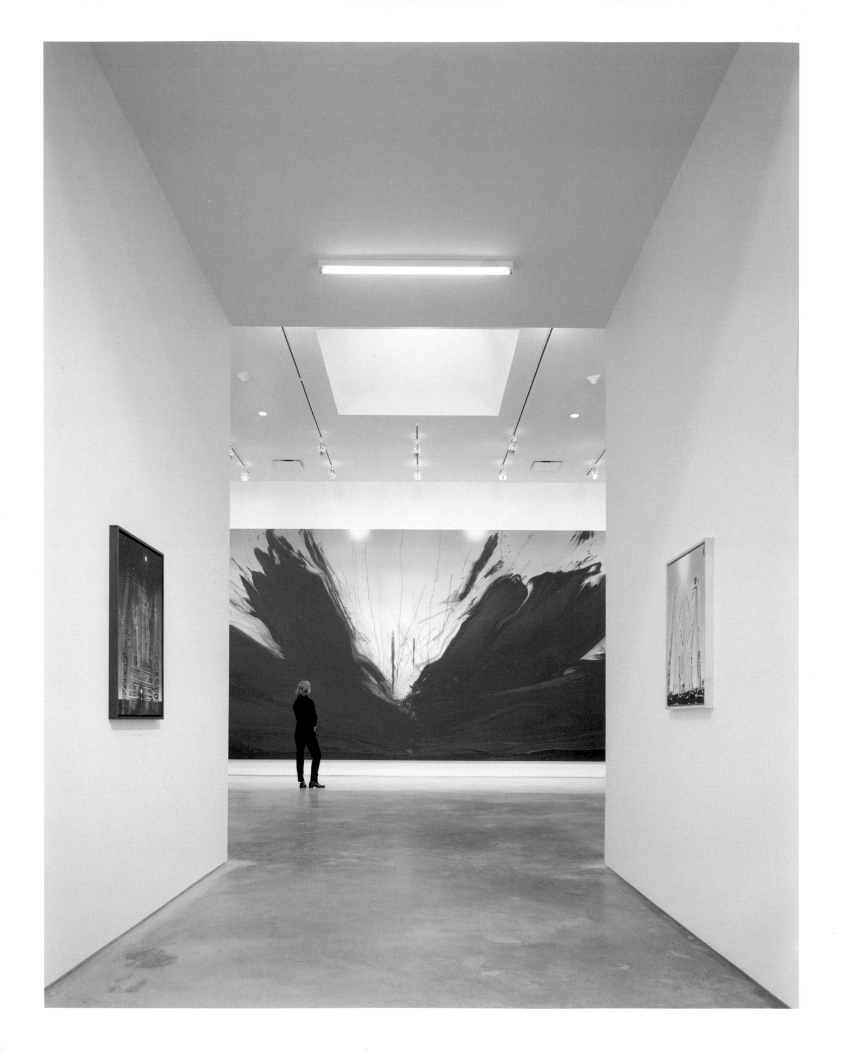

DEBORAH BERKE

FOREWORD BY

AMY HEMPEL

DEBORAH BERKE

TRACY MYERS

YALE UNIVERSITY PRESS
NEW HAVEN AND LONDON

Project directors: Diana Murphy and Miko McGinty
Designed by Miko McGinty assisted by Rita Jules
Printed in Italy

Library of Congress
Cataloging-in-Publication Data

Myers, Tracy, 1957–
  Deborah Berke / by Tracy Myers ; foreword by Amy
Hempel.
      p. cm.
  Includes bibliographical references.
  ISBN 978-0-300-13439-1 (cloth : alk. paper)
  1. Berke, Deborah—Criticism and interpretation.
I. Berke, Deborah. II. Title.
  NA737.B468M94 2008
  720.92—dc22

2008018985

A catalogue record for this book is available from the British Library.

The paper in this book meets the guidelines for permanence and durability of
the Committee on Production Guidelines for Book Longevity of the Council
on Library Resources.

10 9 8 7 6 5 4 3 2 1

Contents

Deborah Berke: "The Ambush of the Ordinary"

Amy Hempel

Deborah Berke leaves out all the right things—things that scream "I" instead of "eye."[1] She overturns the expected: Concrete becomes opulent! White warms a room! Extravagance in her design is found not in lavish additions, but in the use of space, in the scale. She understands the need for logic, and her designs are logical on their own terms. In every project she does, you find what the critic Sven Birkerts calls "the ambush of the ordinary." He is describing a practice that "has more to do with the quality of attention paid than the thing paid attention to."

In the words of Berke's friend the writer A. M. Homes, her work "is about precision and purity and the essential elements—a kind of clarity that is uplifting."

For fifteen years I lived on the East End of Long Island in an Arts and Crafts cottage not far from the ocean. It needed everything, and had a spectacularly ugly kitchen with matte black countertops of a calcified spongy material. Other rooms needed to be redone, but it was this kitchen I was most eager to forget when I enlisted my friend Deborah Berke to redesign and rebuild the downstairs.

I was sickened by the sight of opened walls with dangling wires. I could not watch the demolition that prefigured the rehabbed house. I could not visualize something that was not already there. But when it was over, I saw that the specificity of Deborah's decisions was every-where pleasing and exactly right. She put a wood floor in the kitchen, the planks stained as dark as possible with ebony paint mixed in. The countertops were fashioned from fireslate in a shade called "graphite." New cabinets were a subtle blue-gray with plain round brushed-nickel pulls. She had factored in the southern exposure of the windows over the sinks to keep it from looking too dark.

I loved it. The house had lost none of the original Arts and Crafts character, yet was immeasurably better in every way.

In those years I spent a lot of time at the house Deborah designed and built for her family two towns over. I remember her excitement at drawing up the plans, and I remember feeling sympathy for what I thought must be such pressure—the knowledge that the result would additionally send a strong signal about her aesthetics and ability. But pressure was not what prompted her design. The result was so clean and mindful of where it was that I felt I was inside and out at the same time. Space, scale, and light were conjoined to make a person breathe deeper. It worked for kids in wet bathing suits tramping through the kitchen, and it worked for an elegant Christmas Eve dinner for eighteen.

Recently I spoke with our friend Benjamin Taylor, a writer, about Deborah Berke's unerring eye. He said, "Hers is an aesthetic that nature pioneered but she brings to perfection." I reminded him of a particularly glorious evening at her house, and asked if he could say what Deborah had done that made us feel both comfortable and elated there. He quoted Primo Levi in *The Periodic Table*: "There have been centuries in which 'beauty' was identified with adornment, the superimposed, the frills; but it is probable that they were deviant epochs and that the true beauty, in which every century recognizes itself, is found in upright stones, ships' hulls, the blade of an ax, the wing of a plane."

And in style that is always in style.

NOTE
1. The "I"/"eye" notion in this piece was inspired by an observation made by Patricia Hampl in *Blue Arabesque: A Search for the Sublime* (Orlando: Harcourt, 2006).

Here and Now

Deborah Berke

Reviewing projects for inclusion in this book, I could not help but think back on their creation, and the influences—internal and external—that helped shape them. The work featured here, twenty-one projects out of nearly two hundred designed since I started practicing more than twenty-five years ago, reflects an evolution in my thinking over those twenty-five years, although the majority have been done in the last decade.

Taking a second look at projects, with the perspective offered by time and distance, is cause for me to consider what it is I think, or believe, about architecture. Ten years ago, I was deeply engaged in the concept of the everyday in architecture. This philosophy of embracing and learning from that which is not expressly constructed through high culture or self-conscious design was crucial to my development as an architect and as a teacher. The results are evident in my work of that period, as well as most explicitly in the book I co-edited with my dear friend and colleague Steven Harris, *Architecture of the Everyday*. What I was trying to do through my buildings was see if it were possible to make an architecture of exceptional everydayness.

However, the irony of being the poster child for the anonymity associated with the everyday was not lost on me; nor were, as the 1990s unfolded into the new century, the limitations of a philosophy based on the status quo. The evolution of my thinking is less a case of no longer believing in the everyday and more a case of the everyday itself transforming under the impact of our hyper-accelerated, mass-mediated civilization. The world that has replaced the former everyday world is no less authentic (how can it be anything but authentically what it is?) than what I was initially inspired by and drawn to, but it is no longer everyday in the way that I once used the word. We, the world of architecture, and it, the everyday, have become too deeply self-aware, imitative, global. Everyday architecture may still be anonymous in its making—maybe even more so as culture becomes ever more placeless and production ever more "offshore"—but it is no longer local in its references. It has specific and identifiable attributes, but they are now not specific to a place or a people. Today I am more inspired by the contradictions of this new everyday than moved to emulate it.

That an architecture of the everyday is no longer my primary concern is also the result of changes in the world of architecture. Architecture's full ascendancy to celebrity status, which began a decade ago or more, has reached a level previously unimaginable, I would suppose, even to those who are now at the pinnacle of this phenomenon. How the individual architect is treated, regarded, respected is of little relevance to my thoughts, although the celebrity of a few has most definitely improved the conditions for all architects. However, the way architecture itself continues to be produced and experienced is of enormous interest, and concern, within the context of this phenomenon. I find many of the buildings born of this condition to be bombastically present yet sadly disengaged from their physical situation. My instinct is to suggest that these signature pieces of celebrity architecture each require much more local distortion and a much less legible signature. What I am proposing is an architecture of a far more nuanced signature shaped, above all, by local conditions.

As I have continued to make architecture during the process of making this book, I have recognized an evolving tendency in my work, the philosophical underpinnings of which have grown out of the proposal put forth above. I will call this position "local knowledge," or the "here and now." This philosophy suggests that architecture must strive to be both of its place and of its time. By "of its place" I do not mean that the architect must be local, but rather that the architecture itself must be, foremost in all of its creative criteria, bound to and grounded in its site. I am interested in an architecture so grounded in its site that it can be nowhere else.

Site-specificity emphasizes the importance of particulars of place and denies interchangeability even in today's global context. "Interchangeable" so often means a dumbing-down, a one-size-fits-all approach. If something can work everywhere/anywhere, this is only because it has reduced places to their most common elements at the expense of their unique ones.

While the notion of things being of a place was once called "vernacular," that word has come to convey—at least in architecture—quaint, old-fashioned, or nostalgic. My desire for buildings to be of a place is not that they be quaint, old-fashioned, or nostalgic, but that they be anchored. This quality is the antidote to so many places being placeless, interchangeable, and unrecognizable while also being completely familiar. In other words, it is, paradoxically, placelessness that has become all too familiar today. I believe that architecture still has the capacity to challenge this, through its own qualities.

My philosophical position no doubt stems in part from my love of New York City. I love all cities, but New York City above all confirms my belief in the power of the everyday place to be absolutely unique. I love the New York City of grime and confusion, of trestles and bridges and streets and streets of anonymous buildings, just as I exult in the new New York City of glass and more glass. New York has taught me that a building can be an icon without being a monument. I do not at all long for it to be as it was, but I do not want it to lose the bits that remind us daily that it is a working city. I strongly object to the obliteration of the things, old or new, that make this place this place alone, that distinguish it as a place from any other. It is not that I am nostalgic for the New York City of a certain era. I simply like the feeling New York City inevitably gives me of knowing where I am. And that desire applies to everywhere.

I believe in the power of architecture not to transform but to underscore, highlight, and direct. We need not only to build of a place, but to build in an effort to enhance and underscore the nature of that place. We need to do so because this is the most resistant, dig-in-your-heels response to banal, uncaring placelessness and the obliteration of the here and now. Reasserting the here and now, which is the antidote to placelessness and homogeneity, demands absolutely that one avoid predictability. To bring out the here, something might have to be quite unexpected, jarring us into the moment, asserting the now. Today I believe in both the here and the now, the here being someplace very deeply specific, the now being an architecture of today, totally responsible in its making. A building that can say what here is will also imply what there is, and it can do so without rhetorical posturing.

If this were a manifesto written for architects, it would start boldly and stridently. Make no buildings that are not anchored in their place. They can be made of anything you wish, and in any way you wish, but once they are complete, you are gone and they must be more of the place and less of you. This does not mean they cannot be totally recognizable as yours, it just means that they would not be complete if they were anywhere else.

This is local knowledge; this is what I am calling the "here and now."

PARK PAVILION

A POTENT SITE

DEBORAH BERKE & PARTNERS ARCH.

A QUIET GREEN AMID EXTRAORDINARY TREES

THE SITE FOR AN EXTRAORDINARY RESPONSE

CONCAVITY

A FLOATING PLANE; NOTHING ON CEILING NO LIGHTS, MR, MISC.— AN ISLAND. LUMINOUS, REFLECTIVE

PROGRAMS:

1. ...WITH DISTINCT FORMAL NEEDS

2. ...REQUIRING WIDE-OPEN SPACE

3. ...'BACK-OF-HOUSE' SPACES

AN EXHIBITION SPACE FOR SMALL OBJECTS, OR WORKS ON PAPER

A SPACE FOR A COCKTAIL RECEPTION FOR 100 PEOPLE

A LECTURE SPACE, OR SPACE FOR A READING; A MUSIC SPACE TO SEAT 60-120 PEOPLE

A CLASSROOM FOR A SCHOOL-GROUP PROJECT

AN INDOOR VENUE FOR 'KIDS FEST'

AN 'ANCHOR' FOR A NEW ENTRANCE TO THE PARK

PROGRAMS WITH DISTINCT FORMAL NEEDS

TALL WHERE NARROW

READING

TIERED SEATING

MODULAR EXHIBITION PANELS CLIP TO STRUCTURE

BROAD WHERE WIDE

WORKSHOP

AN INDOOR PAVILION FROM WHICH TO VIEW THE PARK

AN INDOOR PAVILION FROM WHICH TO VIEW "MAD. SQ. ART" INSTALLATIONS

AN 'EXALTED' SPACE; HIGH-CEILINGED AND SPACIOUS, ITSELF A 'WORK OF ART'

ALL SERVICES COME FROM FLOOR, VIA BASEMENT, THROUGH A LUMINOUS SMOOTH CEILING — REFLECTING THE SHIMMERING LIGHT OF THE PARK; 'DAPPLED'

PROGRAMS THAT REQUIRE WIDE-OPEN SPACE

ENTER   KITCHEN/ MISC.

INFORMATION DESK
COAT CHECK
STAFF BATHROOM
KITCHENETTE

STORAGE FOR:
DISPLAY DEVICES
CHAIRS
LECTERN
TABLES
ELECTRONICS

MECHANICAL SPACES

PARK FUNCTIONS:
SIGNAGE
BULLETIN BOARD & TAKE-AWAYS

CONSOLIDATE EXISTING ELECTRICAL VAULTS IN BASEMENT

Arresting Architecture

Tracy Myers

Introduction

Deborah Berke makes good buildings.

In more than twenty-five years of practice, Berke and her associates have produced an extraordinarily consistent body of work that is defined by its tectonic coherence, meticulous attention to detail, and an attitude of deference to its inhabitants. Free of gratuitous gestures and convoluted ideology, the work is the product of rigorous analysis and editing of ideas and is grounded in the conviction that architecture is not an end in itself, but a setting for life's activities. Berke builds fluid yet arresting spaces that are deeply rewarding, impressing not through the assertiveness of her ego, but with their restraint and grace. The integrity of Berke's work—the successful melding of parts into a "harmonious, intact whole"[1]—endows it with an almost palpable serenity. Berke's projects give one great satisfaction, yielding the sensation that the space or building is just as it ought to be and, at the same time, inducing a subtle awareness that *someone* made it so.

That Berke has sustained a high level of constancy across close to two hundred projects is particularly noteworthy in light of the multiple types of projects she has designed and the varied scales at which she has worked. Although she earned initial renown for renovations of lofts and commercial spaces in New York City, Berke in fact has a broad-based practice that is typologically diverse, including commercial, residential, civic, educational, and other institutional projects. Since 2000, new construction and larger-scale nonresidential work have comprised a growing proportion of her oeuvre, and her geographical reach has expanded well beyond the New York area. Demonstrating equal ease and facility at the scale of a small house and a campus master plan, Berke and her associates at Deborah Berke & Partners Architects have amassed a rich portfolio of work that is deft and solid, and reveals a deep desire to take on new typologies and design challenges.

It is a body of work that also resists stylistic typecasting. Although the reductivist elegance and subtlety of her best-known work earned her the title "Miss Minimalism" from one journalist,[2] Berke also has designed numerous projects in a mode that she describes as "pitched-roof modernism," reflecting a synthesis of vernacular-inspired form and modernist austerity. While the term "pitched-roof modernism" would seem to be internally contradictory or suggest indecision, the open-minded approach to form-making that it implies accounts to a large degree for the allure of the firm's work. Deliberately eschewing a preconceived set of assumptions or moves, Berke allows the parameters of each architectural problem to elicit her creative response. She acknowledges her admiration of Louis Kahn and Eero Saarinen,

Submission to an invited competition for the Museum for African Art and Edison Schools Headquarters, New York, New York, 1999–2000

Wallpaper*, September/October 1996

Crestview Lane House, Sagaponack, New York, 2001–4

48 Bond Street, New York, New York, 2006–8

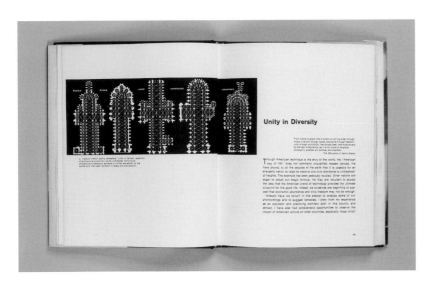

Plans of French Gothic cathedrals. From Walter Gropius, "Unity in Diversity," in *Apollo in the Democracy*, 1968

and the firm's rejection of stylistic dogma reflects both Kahn's respect for the formal integrity of each building and Saarinen's spirit of project-directed invention. Berke's agile mind seeks the appropriately specific resolution of program, opportunity, constraints, and imagination in each project, and the totality of her work reveals the gradual unfolding of an intellectual path.

What unifies Berke's oeuvre is the practice of bringing together in each project the insights, experiences, tactics, and ideas that will produce a unique architectural work that is "right." This quality of "inevitability," as Berke describes it, does not result in predictability, however. The vigilant avoidance of conventions—her own as well as those of the profession at large—often produces a sense of surprise that causes one to take notice of the finished work. The coherence of Berke's designs, in other words, is the consequence of a consistent strategy rather than a set of unvarying practices.

This argument situates Berke's work within a distinct aspect of the modernist tradition. My assertion that it is a form of action rather than particular physical characteristics that defines Berke's work, and the corollary that the regular enactment of this form of action brings coherence to her diverse oeuvre, instantly call to mind Walter Gropius's philosophy of modern architecture. Gropius adamantly opposed the terms "Modern Style" and "International Style" and the homogeneity they implied, contending that modernism was an approach to architectural problem-solving rather than a checklist of the formal attributes a contemporary building should possess.[3] Gropius also repeatedly used the phrase "unity in diversity," which he thought of as both democracy's principal characteristic and a state that contemporary architecture could—and should attempt to—attain.[4] The caption for an image in an essay on this subject shows a series of plans of French Gothic cathedrals that concisely makes his case: "Unity in variety: repetition of architectural elements [in varied buildings] simultaneously achieves a unified expression of the period and individual variation in scale and composition."[5] This is precisely Berke's achievement.

There is of course no small irony in the fact that American architecture under the sway of modernism became exactly the "multiplication of a fixed idea of 'Gropius architecture'" against which the architect cautioned.[6] The association is apt, however, in the realization of Berke's work, if not in its philosophical intention. Another aspect of this connection relates to the essential humbleness of the typologies of early modernism—housing, hospitals, schools—and of much of Berke's oeuvre. That modesty, expressed in Berke's comparatively light touch, is consonant with her respect for the intrinsic qualities of the architectural object—be it a building, a light socket, or an element of any scale between the two.

In the early 1990s, this sensibility led Berke to articulate a theoretical position on what she called "the architecture of the everyday." Inspired by the way in which vernacular forms genuinely intrigue her, Berke offered up her notion of the everyday as a corrective to the growing fetishization of the stars in the architectural firmament. However, rather than resorting to the glib and alternately diluted and overly literal recycling of vernacular motifs that emerged in the wake of Robert Venturi and Denise Scott Brown's polemic,[7] she embraced the authentically ordinary: generic and anonymous materials, banal and common building forms, and what she described as "the crude, the vulgar or [the] visceral." Berke argued for an architecture that, among other things, honors daily life and embodies the symbolic attributes of monumentality without assuming the scale of a monument. She asserted, finally, that an everyday architecture can be neither strictly defined nor predicted nor, one might deduce, forced into being.[8]

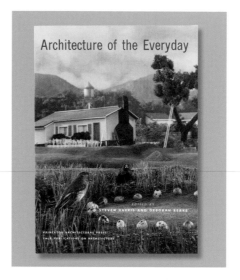

Cover of Steven Harris and Deborah Berke, eds., *Architecture of the Everyday*, 1997

Not surprisingly, this strong and earnest statement of an anti-aesthetic elicited at least one critique of Berke's work in the form of a kind of checklist, as if to assess not only the extent to which she adhered to her philosophy, but also its validity.[9] That analysis, however, missed the fact that what Berke was urging was a fundamental rethinking of architectural aspirations:

> In the early '90s, the idea of the everyday was radical in a number of ways. It was radical as a compositional inspiration, it was radical as a materials palette, it was radical in asking, "What programs do you embrace?" and in saying, "Let's look at the motel, the suburban house, or the factory." To me, the "everyday" isn't reducible to buying materials at Home Depot. It's much more about what part of the built landscape you look at for your inspiration, what part of cities you find interesting, what programs you embrace and want to take on as an architect. A large part of that is the workplace, and that is not a program type that most design firms were interested in taking on in the '90s. Maybe they would be now, but certainly, at that time, nobody else was doing it; nobody else cared.[10]

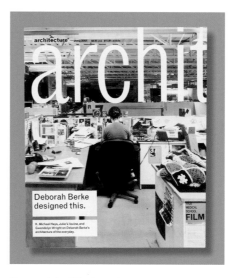

Cover of *Architecture*, June 2001

In the past decade, the democratization of design has resulted in a massive shift in popular taste and a corresponding inversion of what constitutes "the everyday," and Berke's polemic no longer rings as

Gymnasium, The MacDuffie School, Springfield, Massachusetts, 2006 (unbuilt). An upper translucent volume created by continuous clerestory glass contrasts with the more contextual fieldstone base. The high thermal mass of the masonry walls and the building's abundant daylight support the school's environmental goals.

revolutionary. Berke's approach has evolved beyond the everyday, which had become inadequate for containing the breadth of the firm's architectural interests. The subversive attitude embodied by the idea of the everyday remains a part of the firm's philosophical DNA, however. It is a subtle subversion of the architectural status quo that is expressed formally, not through ostentatious and ultimately datable moves but through the unexpected gesture, in work that aims for rightness, a calculated degree of visibility, balance, and repose. Products of the delicate equilibrium Berke maintains between asserting and relinquishing her presence, these qualities account for the exceptional sensations her buildings provoke.

The range that is the outcome of Berke's nimbleness raises the question of what connects projects as diverse as those presented here. The easy answer to this question is that the absence of a single idea across all projects—of a signature style—*is* the meta-narrative of Berke's oeuvre.[11] There is an ambiguity in this statement, however, that goes to the heart of the prickly challenge of coming to conclusions about a body of work that refuses to be pegged. The constant in Berke's work is an attempt to make visible the *evidence* of an architect's hand in such a way that the *identity* of the hand is not instantly knowable. At the same time, Berke and her partners take a certain pleasure in the idea that a person might encounter one of their projects and realize that architects had intervened but be unable to put a finger on what, exactly, they had done.[12] Berke wants to have it both ways, creating work that is discernibly the product of design yet still somewhat elusive. This, of course, raises additional questions: If the design hand is so unobtrusive, how is it to be understood? If each project evolves through a singular process of iteration, critique, and reiteration, what does the work collectively have in common?

The force of Berke's work lies in the fact that each project stands on its own terms. Berke acknowledges that at the level of form, compositional strategies recur in her designs: asymmetry, for example, or the interpenetration of spatial volumes in section. Similarly, certain types of details or ways of using materials appear in multiple projects: a warm palette of woods, perhaps, or the juxtaposition of cladding materials such that they simultaneously clarify individual forms and unify them. Considered in quantity and over time, Berke's projects reveal associations or commonalities that, in their complexity and mutability, call to mind a kind of kinetic three-dimensional matrix. A basin of Manhattan schist in one project reappears in a different form of bathroom fixture in another; a breezeway shot through one house

Sospiro Canal House, Fort Lauderdale, Florida, 2001–4. View of entrance, showing juxtaposition of mahogany and Keys coral stone

Mercer Street Loft No. 1, New York, New York, 1996–98. Bathroom trough sink and tub (reflected in mirror)

to frame a view echoes the single outsize window in the façade of a gallery building; a wall of closets is rendered in plywood in an industrial workshop and textured oak in university faculty housing. While the dots can be connected in many ways, the work never gives the impression that the architects have simply defaulted to a familiar formal position or dipped into a bag of reliable tricks. Nor could one extrapolate from past work to anticipate DBPA's response to a given site or program. All the same, there is an ineffable *something* that suffuses the firm's work, allowing it to cohere as a complete body.

That something is related to what the firm calls a "sense of rightness," a feeling of "compositional arrest" and stability, that results from a balance of elements. An important aspect of rightness is the use of compositional elements in unexpected ways: an asymmetrical organization of volumes, a window that appears to be out of place, cladding of a façade with a material that is not typically found on exteriors. While the notion of rightness is invoked here in relation to compositional strategy, it is the key to understanding Berke's work as a whole. Her buildings are carefully calibrated meditations on visibility that rely on a discourse between a subtle hand and more evidently designed elements. Components that anchor her buildings in place and time—that express the "here and now" of which Berke writes— come together with more conspicuously visible elements, resulting in rich, engaging compositions. Berke's buildings may elicit a kind of double take—the surveying glance, followed by the uncanny perception that something very particular has been designed.

Berke's rejection of formula and deference to the specificity of each project's conditions and requirements extend to her pedagogical philosophy. Throughout her career, teaching has complemented practice, and not surprisingly, Berke encourages in her students the same flexibility of approach, capacity for unsparing analysis, and widely informed point of view that she brings to her own work. Much as her interest in the ordinariness of the everyday anticipated the eventual apotheosis of consumer culture to a design opportunity, Berke's studios have probed the interstices of conventional architectural education, examining typologies like the suburban house long before they became popular objects of scrutiny. Regarded by her students as an incisive, acute, and generous critic, she also is esteemed for cultivating their creative individuality rather than nudging them toward a particular methodology, language, or architectural identity. Indeed, Berke's goal is "to allow my students to find their own voice. I teach them how to be their own best critics, as that is the skill they'll need to make buildings themselves someday."

Opposite: Washington Square Village faculty housing, New York University, New York, New York, 2003–4

Reedy Creek Fire Station 2-B, Lake Buena Vista, Florida, 2007–present. While straightforward in form, this emergency services building is inspired by the purposefully extra-ordinary color of the department's fire trucks. "Safety" lime-yellow panels, shaped with a subtly bossed profile and finished in porcelain enamel, turn a utilitarian structure into a celebratory and arresting object visible from the nearby highway.

The humility that accounts for the lightness of Berke's hand in her design and teaching is manifest in a characteristically complex way in relation to the matter of gender. It is perhaps inevitable that the gender discourse is invoked with respect to Berke, given her success as a practitioner and professor, and the persistent under-representation of women in the field. Berke is reluctant to engage this discussion, in part because she feels that she is not yet able to attain the distance and level of objectivity necessary to make a judgment about what role, if any, her gender has played in her career. When pressed, she acknowledges that she has been considered a model for young women architects or faculty members. "Sometimes," she says, "people who are accomplished in their own right come to me and say, 'You inspired me. I heard about you, and I thought I could do it, too.'"

While she appreciates these sentiments, Berke thinks of her accomplishments as, simply, the expression of a self-imposed imperative to make architecture that is "of its time and place." Elizabeth Eakins, a client for two projects, uses terms such as "honorable" in speaking about Berke.[13] Eakins does not mean to suggest a retrenchment by Berke to some uncritical position of naïveté. Rather, what she has zeroed in on are the clear-sightedness, effacement of ego, and constancy of imagination that for more than twenty-five years have enabled Berke to make *good buildings* here and now.

NOTES

1. Damian Cox, Marguerite La Caze, and Michael Levine, "Integrity," in Edward N. Zalta, ed., *The Stanford Encyclopedia of Philosophy (Fall 2005 Edition)*, http://plato.stanford.edu/archives/fall2005/entries/integrity/.

2. Tyler Brûlé, "The Making of Miss Minimalism," *Wallpaper** (Sept./Oct. 1996), 19–21.

3. Walter Gropius, "Architecture at Harvard University," *Architectural Record* (May 1937), 9–10.

4. Walter Gropius, "Unity in Diversity," in *Apollo in the Democracy: The Cultural Obligation of the Architect* (New York: McGraw-Hill, 1968), 20ff.

5. Ibid., 20.

6. Gropius, "Architecture at Harvard University," 10.

7. Robert Venturi, Denise Scott Brown, and Steven Izenour, *Learning from Las Vegas* (Cambridge, Mass.: MIT Press, 1972).

8. Steven Harris and Deborah Berke, eds., *Architecture of the Everyday* (New York: Princeton Architectural Press, 1997), 222–25, my emphasis.

9. K. Michael Hays, Julie Iovine, and Gwendolyn Wright, "Exceptionally Ordinary," *Architecture* (June 2001), 90–101.

10. Deborah Berke, Maitland Jones, and Marc Leff, interview by the author, Oct. 16, 2006.

11. Ibid.

12. Ibid.

13. Elizabeth Eakins, interview by the author, Jan. 27, 2006.

Site and the Body

Site and the Body

Site. It surely is to the architect what the blank page is to the writer, the empty canvas to the painter: the sublime locus of promise and opportunity and, at the same time, constraints and obstacles. Both object and subject, it is the source of the treasured view as well as the element around which architectural aspirations are molded. The first glimpse of the site, the first footfall on it, sets in motion the eventual unfolding of architectural meaning. That an architect can look at a vacant site and envision what will be built there and how it will lie on the land is slightly wondrous.

If site is the obvious point of departure for architecture, however, it is worth considering precisely what the *act* of siting amounts to. More interesting than the question of how the orientation and the relationship of a building's parts affect one's physical engagement with a place is the abstract matter of the *phenomenological* consequences of locating a building in a particular way. Thinking about siting as the determinant of one's perceptual connections to a place or a building calls to mind a case described by neurologist Oliver Sacks in his book *The Man Who Mistook His Wife for a Hat and Other Clinical Tales*. In "The Disembodied Lady," Sacks writes about a young woman who suddenly and completely lost her sense of her body parts' position in relation to each other. As the patient described it, proprioception is "the way the body sees itself"; without it her body was "blind," and her limbs would behave in contrary and disparate ways. To compensate for this severe neurological deficit, the woman taught herself to anchor her body in space by using visual cues.[1]

Considered in this context, siting is essentially an act of architectural proprioception, mooring spatial perception by fixing physical relationships. Whether these relationships position the building as object or subject—that is, as the thing that is inhabited or the thing that is viewed—they are, at bottom, what enable us to situate ourselves in space. Deborah Berke situates projects as both objects and subjects. One's "position-sense" is thus formed as a mediation between siting and composition. Determinations about the positioning of a building on the land are informed by careful regard for the particularity of the site's conditions, rather than an a priori idea of form, and Berke's field of vision on approaching a site is wide:

> I think that the architect and the client have to right away
> get past understanding property lines as the definition of site.
> When you start a project—assuming that it's a freestanding
> building—what you're given is the outline of the thing your
> client owns. But of course, the space in which you will be able

Housing Redevelopment Scheme, Forest Hills, New York, 2003 (unbuilt). This seven-acre former industrial site abuts a small-scale residential neighborhood on one side, with large-scale commercial development and an abandoned, forested railroad embankment on the other two sides. Berke's strategy of mediation operates in two ways: articulation of each of the three residential buildings as a block floating above an architecturally and functionally distinct pedestal mitigates the big shift in scale; and a lushly landscaped garden on the plaza effects a transition between the constructed environment and the railroad embankment.

Irwin Union Bank, Columbus, Indiana, 2004–6. View from adjoining parking lot

to appreciate the thing you're going to make is rarely defined by those property lines. You have to look at other elements, whether it's the presence of the building next door or a line of trees or the ocean or a dune or a hollow, many of which may not be on the property. The first step in my consideration of all sites is to back *way* up, to look at the property from much farther away, much farther down the road, much farther up above, to see what else is in it. And to imagine what could happen in the future that's beyond your control. I think you have to be aware of future possibilities and that the land will change over time.

While Berke's description of her initial take on a site addresses pragmatic considerations of boundaries and actual and possible contexts, embedded within it is an implicit understanding of the proprioceptive implications of siting. The projects in this section suggest several approaches Berke has taken to shaping the connection between a building and its place—in Sacks's terms, one's "position-sense" in relation to the building.[2]

Where a site is formless or otherwise thwarts an effort to secure spatial and perceptual moorings, Berke has employed strategies that impart a sense of fixity. The site of her branch for Irwin Union Bank, in Columbus, Indiana, is the ill-defined swirl of a strip mall, crossed by randomly laid roads serving a scattershot configuration of big-box retailers. Berke's building, a luminous glass box stacked perpendicularly on a simple brick volume, is a literal beacon at the end of an indistinct path, a kind of stake in the heart of the cluttered context that sharply conveys the message, "Here is your destination." The firm took the opposite approach in developing a master plan for the similarly amorphous condition at Marlboro College. Located in rural Vermont, the campus of the tiny private college had evolved haphazardly over fifty years, with buildings dispersed widely across the campus. Moreover, the area that should have been the psychological core of the campus was dominated by parking lots. Berke proposed clearing the campus's heart of the objects that made it unrecognizable—principally, cars. Whereas in Columbus the construction of a building establishes a center, here the creation of a void defines the core. In both cases, Berke's intervention resulted in a new set of orienting relationships between place and user.

In other projects, the stability of one's "position-sense" is mediated by both siting and composition. A house in Sagaponack, in eastern Long Island, is built on a deep dune overlooking the Atlantic Ocean. Because the town's zoning regulations strictly limit building heights,

Crestview Lane House, Sagaponack, New York, 2001–4. Approach from land side and view from breezeway across the dune the architects' challenge in designing the two-story house was to maximize the stunning view of the ocean from both floors. The design problem was resolved in part in section: several changes in elevation accommodate the site, and the ground floor is lifted to provide views across the dune. The navigability of the house— one's relationship to its spaces—thus is, in essence, a matter of one's relationship to the views. This is more dramatically manifest in the experience of approaching the house from the land side, where an aperture cut through the building frames a bit of sky, drawing one up the slight rise toward the dune and into the house in a clear but constantly shifting progression of proprioceptive moments. The same compositional gesture is employed in a house in Warren, Connecticut, that sits parallel to the ridge of a high hill offering a wide, unimpeded view to the west. While the opening again frames a view, the impact here is very different from that at the Sagaponack house. Whereas at the latter the aperture has the effect of concentrating or gathering the site's spatial energy to the house, in the Connecticut house it acts to release and disperse that energy, opening the visual field such that one's physical experience of the view is somewhat centrifugal.

The strategy that entails perhaps the most direct establishment of a perceptual connection between a building and its locale is what one might describe as drawing a bead on a site. One of Berke's earliest projects is a house in Indianapolis that occupies a dramatically sloping site at the edge of the White River. Indianapolis was laid out by Alexander Ralston, an apprentice to Pierre L'Enfant, on the same hub-and-spoke principle on which L'Enfant planned Washington, D.C. At the hub of Indianapolis is the state Soldiers' and Sailors' Monument, and it is in relation to this monument, seven miles away, in the heart of the city, that the main gesture of Berke's house is oriented. The organizing feature of the house, a large "hole" through the main volume, is sited on axis with the monument, which is visible from the property when its trees are bare. This vista holds great personal significance for the home's owner, who developed several projects in downtown Indianapolis and has a great affection for the city. More than simply the location of the owner's residence, the site is part of his psychic geography, and the building's siting truly embodies his relationship to place.

Although the word "site" typically conjures an exterior setting, it also describes a set of interior conditions. Berke imaginatively turns to her advantage the constraints that these conditions almost inevitably entail to construct refined spaces in which site is experienced both literally and in its homonymic sense, as a view. For the American

White River House, Indianapolis, Indiana, 1986–87

Industria Superstudio, New York, New York, 1990–91

GAV, New York, New York, 2004

headquarters of Industria Superstudio, a company that rents space, equipment, and services for fashion photography shoots, Berke converted an auto repair garage built in the 1930s into a suite of studios and supporting facilities. The backbone of the two-story building is an interior ramp, which DBPA exploited as an organizing device, inserting a series of parallel planes to define zones of space. The ramp became the sight line along which these planes reveal themselves as one looks from the top of the ramp down toward the street level. In much the same way that the axial orientation of the Indianapolis house extends the perceptual scope of the property, the ramp at Industria has the effect of an elongated perspective.

Berke employed a different strategy to similar effect in converting a floor of a former printing factory into a showroom and studio for GAV, which developed and designed clothing lines for Calvin Klein and other New York design labels. To bring focus to the open space, Berke enclosed the central row of a grid of columns in a crisp line of closets and inserted a wall behind the neighboring row of columns, creating a dramatic hundred-foot-long corridor. A voluptuous stair is the only punctuation in a perspectively exaggerated path leading from the entrance to a large showroom.

Where the topography of a site offers no inherent opportunities, Berke has on occasion created a topography, in part as a means of "blurring the absolute distinction between the object and the thing it sits on." The firm's submission to the New Housing New York Design Ideas Competition in 2004, for an eleven-acre site on the waterfront in western Queens, proposed mixed-use buildings of various heights interspersed with farmable plots of land, producing a topography of varying scales of public space between the urban fringe of the site and

Food & Shelter: Urban Farming and Affordable Homes, award-winning submission to New Housing New York Design Ideas Competition, 2004. Proposed for a site in Queens, New York, an apartment building with an exterior skin of movable louvers forms the backdrop for an urban farm planted on the parking garage's roof.

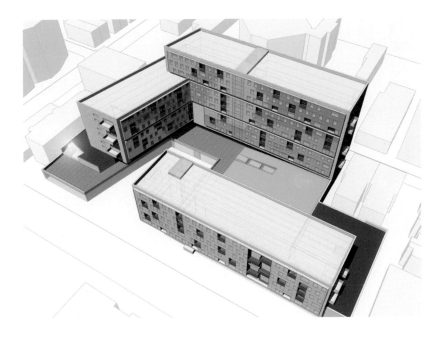

the East River. Interior streets extend into the river as piers, constituting a kind of embrace both formally and by claiming a portion of the river for the site. This gesture has the further effect of changing one's relationship to the site by rupturing its putative limits.

Use of the word "embrace" here is deliberate, suggesting both a physical connection and a notion that the orientation of a building can exert a figurative hold on one. Berke's proposed mixed-use complex for an urban university suggests the dual nature of site. A two-story retail/office block brackets a deep courtyard and forms the plinth for two residential buildings: a bar-shaped building along the street, and a taller L-shaped structure that wraps a corner of the courtyard. The buildings' varying heights and asymmetrical disposition around the outdoor space result in a composition that both anchors and enlivens an otherwise unremarkable street, and the courtyard exerts a pull that draws one into the site.

More than a matter merely of positioning a building within its setting, siting is the first act by which the architect shapes the physical relationships that enable us to understand, literally, our body's place in the world—our *spatial* hold on it. For Berke, this relationship is deeply implicated in the *particularity* of a site—the precise way in which a building is *of* its place. The notion of site-specificity in which Berke's work is grounded is revealed in varied ways in the projects that follow.

NOTES
1. Oliver Sacks, "The Disembodied Lady," in *The Man Who Mistook His Wife for a Hat and Other Clinical Tales* (New York: Summit Books, 1985), 42–52.
2. Ibid., 45.

Walnut Street High-Rise, Philadelphia, Pennsylvania, 2006 (unbuilt)

Irwin Union Bank

Columbus, Indiana
2004–6

Irwin Union Bank has a tradition of building modern, innovative buildings, and Berke's project joins branches designed by Eero Saarinen, Harry Weese, and Kevin Roche, among other architects. Irwin Union Bank's Creekview branch in Columbus, Indiana, is DBPA's second building in Bartholomew County.

The bank occupies a 1.6-acre site in the uniquely American context of a suburban strip mall, which, in this case, includes two gargantuan big-box retail buildings, a multiplex theater, a car wash, a chain Italian restaurant, and the inevitable sea of asphalt parking lots. In the flat natural topography of Columbus, it is these structures that constitute a landscape. Immediately south of the mall is an undeveloped field, providing a curious additional layer of context. The company specifically communicated to Berke its "aspiration to improve the neighborhood by designing to a higher level of quality than the surrounding buildings without blowing the budget."[1]

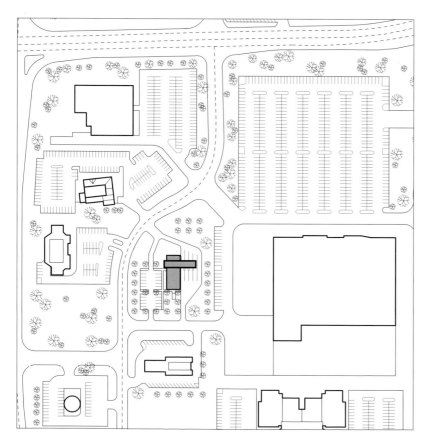

Berke's Irwin Union Bank is situated in an amorphous setting occupied by disconnected buildings that bear little scalar relationship to each other.

Recognizing that the primary perspective on the 4,000-square-foot bank would be experienced from cars traveling on the nearby road, DBPA sought a strategy that would ensure the building's visibility amid this jumbled setting, despite its modest size. This was accomplished through the simple but bold design gesture of floating a translucent glass "light box" above a structure of brick and Indiana limestone. The carefully calculated, asymmetrical relationship of these taut volumes produces a subtle tension that both arrests one's attention and, in its directness, offers respite from the mall's visual and aural noise. A similarly measured approach to the interior results in a fine balance between the physicality of materials and the ethereal illumination admitted by the light box.

NOTE
1. Will Miller, chairman, president, and CEO of Irwin Financial Corp., e-mail to the author, June 19, 2007.

By night, the light box literally acts as a beacon in the barely decipherable mallscape.

The light box is constructed of planks of structural channel glass and metal-deck roofing, which complement the modest elegance of the concrete floor and maple teller station. The use of economical materials allowed Berke to achieve the client's most important goal: "cost-effective creation of a very good design."

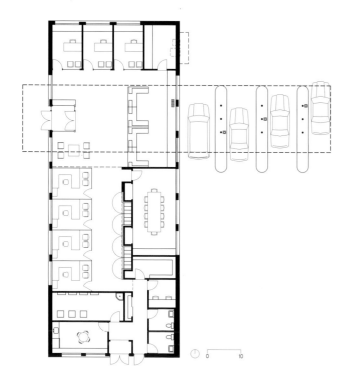

The bank's public operations for customers both on foot and in their cars are contained almost entirely within the zone defined by the light box. Private offices, client consultation spaces, conference rooms, and support spaces are dispersed through the brick-and-limestone volume.

The orthogonal regularity of the bank's interior provides relief from the building's disorderly context. Ovoid light fixtures seem to float in the space, reinforcing the quality of airiness created by the light box.

Berke's design frankly acknowledges drive-through banking as an equal partner to more traditional walk-in banking, rather than treating it as an afterthought.

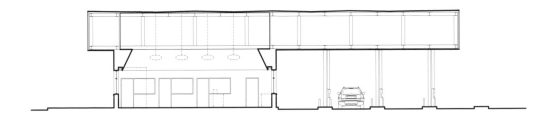

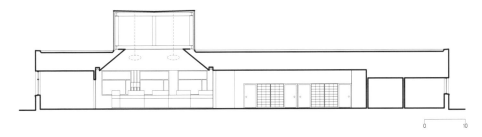

Sections looking north (top) and east (above)

Brick buildings form part of the context from which Berke's design takes its cues. The translucent light box is a moment of transition between the brick volume, which is grounded to its flat site, and the vast sky. As the light box extends over the drive-through lanes, it captures a piece of the landscape, subtly staking the building's claim to its site.

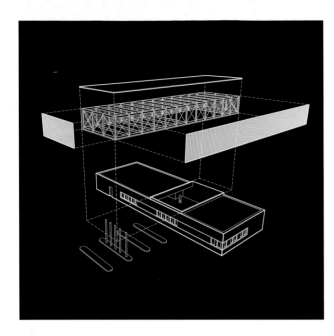

The building's two components are dissimilar in character: a low masonry volume is surmounted by a diaphanous glass-and-steel box.

The asymmetrical disposition of the building's two volumes is expressed on the west side as a short canopy over the bank's entrance, created by a slight extension of the light box beyond the façade.

Rabbit Hill Road Compound

Warren, Connecticut
1998–2000

The Rabbit Hill Road Compound, a 3,000-square-foot weekend retreat with outbuildings in western Connecticut, sits on a north-south axis parallel to the ridge of a site that drops steeply to the west and falls more gently to the east. The house was sited to ensure that it receives maximum exposure to the morning sun; while nestled into the landscape, it is positioned high enough on the hill to capture the expansive vista of rolling farmland. A loosely defined courtyard that encloses a piece of the landscape is formed by the house, garage, and pool house. Landscaped terraces and walls crafted from stone taken from the site extend the immediate precinct of the compound into the landscape.

Composed of three interlocking volumes, the house is approached through the garage, which shields it from the road. The principal volume is a continuous bar that encloses several different sectional conditions and contains most of the program. A full-height screened porch punctures the bar structure, dissolving the distinction between indoors and outdoors and providing an environmentally conscientious alternative to air-conditioning. The house's strong orthogonal character is reinforced by the visual transverse axis set by views east and west from the porch. In a gesture that literally connects the house to its site, Berke created a breakfast terrace on the east side of the house that is anchored by a large rock outcropping.

As one traverses the property, the components of the house resolve in a series of changing parallel and perpendicular relationships. Together, the shedlike volumes and a simple materials palette of galvanized metal roofing, stained cedar shingles and vertical siding, and stucco make the project a disarming combination of modern compositional strategies and vernacular functionalism.

The site plan reveals the varied character of the topography, on which the project's three components (pool and pool house to the west; parking area and garage to the east of these; and the house to the north) impose a strong orthogonal regularity.

View through the garage and across the path to the house's entrance. The mix of materials—standing-seam galvanized metal roofing, and cedar shingles and vertical boards stained a warm gray—imparts a restrained but rewarding sense of texture to the garage's simple form.

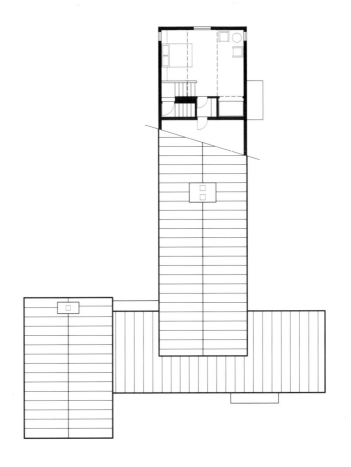

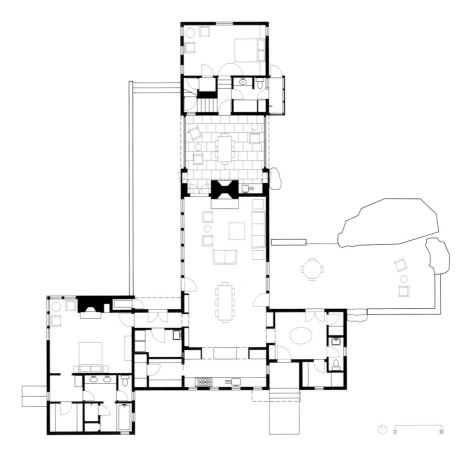

The perspective across the path from the garage (foreground of photograph) to the house divulges the organization of the three volumes: a low "shed" structure containing the entrance to the house is intersected by two two-story volumes—the master suite (left) and the long bar building containing a double-height living room and two-story guest suite.

New random ashlar stone walls define the area occupied by the pool and pool house and establish the western and southern boundaries of the "courtyard" (see site plan).

View through the screened porch from the cocktail terrace on the west side of the house. Interior and exterior become one through the use of a consistent palette of vertical siding, bluestone, and cedar shingles.

The simplicity of two pure volumes viewed from the west, with the master suite at right, belies the complexity of the house's composition.

Darby Lane House

East Hampton, New York
1998–2000

Located on a quiet residential lane in the Georgica section of East Hampton, this 3,400-square-foot house is sited in relation to a group of large, stately trees and in the southernmost corner of the property in order to leave open as large an expanse of the lawn as possible. Although the house is carefully sited well to one side of the property in deference to its natural features, the volumes of which it is composed are organized into a taut configuration that responds to the physical setting. But for a slight dip between one exterior wall of the house and a large existing fir tree, the property was virtually without topography. Landscape architect Margie Ruddick shaped this depression into a sunken garden defined by a low wall of stone slabs. Like other outdoor spaces immediately adjacent to the house, it is oriented so as to establish views, physical paths, or sitting areas between groups of trees.

The Darby Lane House is an assemblage of simple interlocking volumes, clad in understated materials—stucco and weathered cedar—that distinguish and reinforce the volumes' individual geometries. Extensive fenestration at several places in the house diminishes the distinction between indoors and outdoors, producing a quality of luminous composure in the interior. Its elegant natural palette of slate, brick, and shiplap board complement the exterior materials and highlight the building's intimate connection to the earth. The result is a structure that is simultaneously modern and contextual, and completely assimilated into its site.

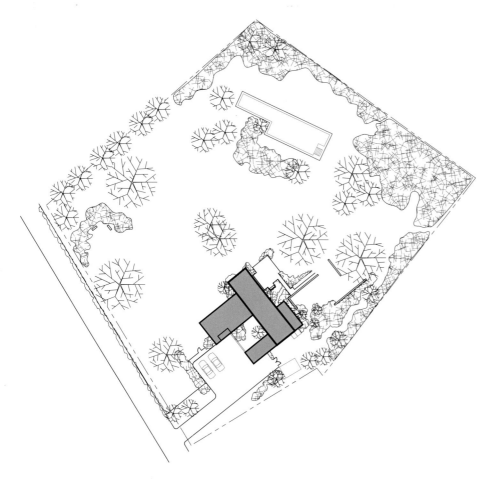

Berke's siting of the house and pool leaves much of the property unoccupied, such that these elements are less an intervention in the landscape than humble lodgers on it. A patio at the rear of the house is the point of departure for one's course across the property to the swimming pool, which is sheltered on one side by a stand of trees.

Although the side of the house that is visible from the narrow public lane is relatively blank and unassuming, the careful composition of its three volumes is discernible instantly on arrival.

The cedar wall of the entry court and garage wraps around the house to become the cladding of the single-height volume containing the library. The sunken garden designed by Margie Ruddick lies just outside the library. The stone of which the low wall is made is also used in walkways.

The brick chimney block appears on the exterior as the hinge between the single-height volume and the entry court. Within the house, the chimney is expressed as a wall containing the fireplace. The building's simple and eloquent palette of brick, cedar, and stucco converges at the entry court.

In contrast to the front of the house, which is closed and private, the garden side of the house is very open, offering expansive views onto the deep lawn.

View from the living/dining area

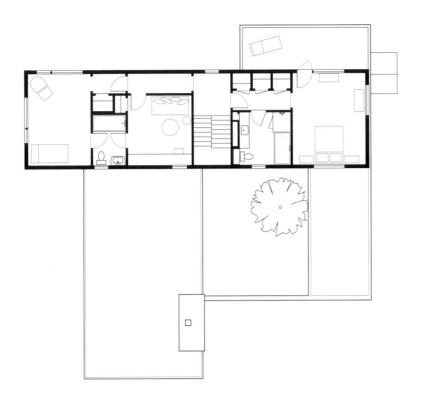

Top: The master suite on the second floor opens onto a deck on the roof of the cedar-clad volume at the rear of the house.

Above: The living/dining area, screened porch, kitchen, library, and guest suite occupy the first floor. The threshold between the living/dining area and the kitchen marks the point of transition in size and orientation of the slate pavers from the public to the private areas of the house. The continuation of the paver pattern from the living space beyond the wall of windows bordering the entry court maintains the integrity of the rectangular volume and establishes the floor as a kind of proscenium for the court.

Kitchen with screened porch beyond

The entry court has the character of an outdoor room. The extension of the gravel surface from the entry court into the parking area underscores the fluidity between the two spaces.

Serkin Center for the Performing Arts

Marlboro College
Marlboro, Vermont
2002–5

In 1997, Berke was commissioned to develop a master plan for Marlboro College, an institution located in the foothills of southern Vermont. Known for a flexible curriculum that allows each of its 330 students to formulate her or his own course of studies, the school is governed through a town meeting system that encourages free exchange among all members of the college community. The campus had developed in a random fashion over its first half-century, and a problem of "parking creep" created a situation in which land was increasingly given over to space for automobiles. While most of the college's buildings and some of the original farmhouse structures were serviceable manifestations of the local vernacular, the campus lacked coherence.

The master plan that evolved out of Berke's comprehensive analysis, undertaken in collaboration with landscape architect Margie Ruddick, proposed a carefully phased series of construction, renovation, and landscape projects. The architects recommended,

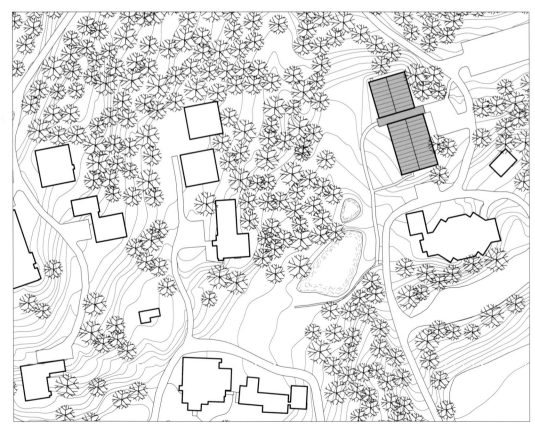

The college's buildings are scattered across the campus. The performing arts center abuts a wooded area and offers a view across the campus from its prominent site.

among other improvements, that the central campus be cleared of parking lots, utility lines, and other visual blight, creating a shared green space that acts as an organizing axis for the entire campus. They also suggested that the college hire different architects to carry out individual building projects; DBPA was awarded the commission for the performing arts center.

The 10,000-square-foot performing arts center is sited on a high point in the academic section of the campus between wetlands and a rocky outcropping and is visible from the center of the campus. Berke composed the building out of two separate volumes—one for the music department and the other for the dance department—that are connected by a shared lobby. The volumes are slightly offset, as if slipping in opposite directions against the spine that links them. This element, which both connects and separates the two principal structures, is a kind of architectonic mirror of the axial void formed by the newly created green. The performing arts center is thus an architectural expression of the campus's spatial condition: a loose assemblage of distinct buildings linked by pockets of communal space.

The music building (foreground) houses a 125-seat auditorium and a digital recording studio in addition to rehearsal space and classrooms. A large studio dominates the dance building (rear); administrative offices are dispersed in the two volumes. The shared lobby, marked by a projecting canopy, is an acoustical buffer between the departments.

Simultaneously contemporary and timeless, the performing arts center's straightforward barnlike volumes are offset not only in plan but also in section, to accommodate a change in elevation. The recessed strip lights in the canopy reinforce the building's clarity and tautness.

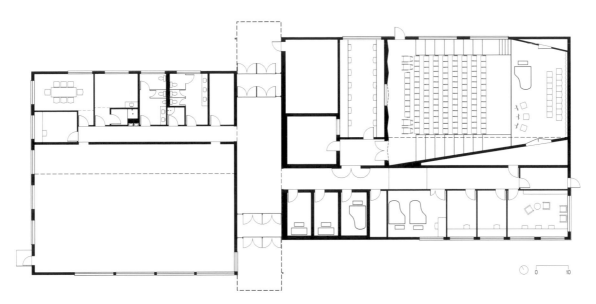

The two components of the building have a reciprocal relationship in plan, with large, open spaces balancing smaller, more private rooms.

Above: While the auditorium's acoustics are tightly controlled, windows allow natural light into the space and give audiences an awareness of the relationship of the building to its site.

Left: Rear view. Volumes are crisply rendered in simple vertical wood siding. A slender column anchors the exposed side of the canopy in both front and rear, visually balancing the composition.

Opposite: Front view, toward the dance studio. The building's roofs are of standing-seam metal, which also sheathes the fascia surfaces of the two canopies.

Above: In the dance studio, generous fenestration provides natural light and the warmth of the southern sun.

Halley Studio

North Hillsdale, New York
1989–92
Berke & McWhorter Architects

Designed for an artist and his family, the Halley Studio joins a modest nineteenth-century red-shingled farmhouse on a property in the Berkshire Mountains of eastern New York State. After analyzing the one-hundred-acre sloping site, Berke & McWhorter Architects, in consultation with the client, proposed a freestanding 1,100-square-foot structure to contain the programmatic components lacking in the original house. The studio nestles into the slope of the hill and lies three hundred feet from the farmhouse, the path between the two buildings determined in part by an existing line of trees.

The architects' scheme configures three distinct volumes around a central staircase. Each contains a single element of the program: a dramatically proportioned painting studio, a screened porch, and a small sleeping suite. The designers gave each volume its own architectural character to reinforce the three-part composition. The studio wing employs the "carpenter's" detailing of a shingled house; the porch is detailed like an open framework of columns; and the modest sleeping quarters are detailed somewhat like a utility shed. In this way, a small building was endowed with greater physical presence than it might ordinarily have had.

Drawing on regional achitecture for both form and language, the architects imparted to this project a sense of the ordinary that is subtly subverted through painstaking attention to detail. The result is a humble but assured building that is at one with its site.

The new structure is reached from the existing house by a long path that follows a stand of trees.

View from the southeast. Subtle variations in cladding and fenestration elicit a double take that reveals the building's deceptive simplicity. The studio (center) is clad in shingles, while the guesthouse (far right) is sheathed in vertical board. Windows are set flush in the guesthouse but are deeply recessed in the studio.

The open, public character of the screened porch (left) contrasts with the reticent, private nature of the studio (right). The flat terrain on this side of the house gives no indication of the change in elevation that is accommodated on the other side of the building.

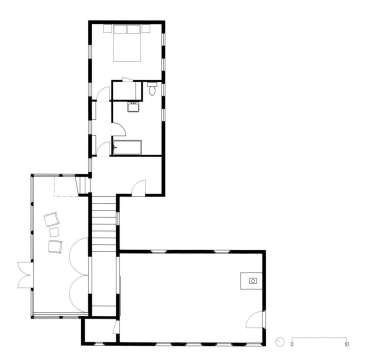

First-floor plan. The three components—screened porch (left), guesthouse (top), and studio (right)—converge on the central hall and staircase.

Carefully nuanced details in the studio—asymmetrical placement of the door's intermediate rail and double-hung windows of four lights over one—throw the spare design into high relief.

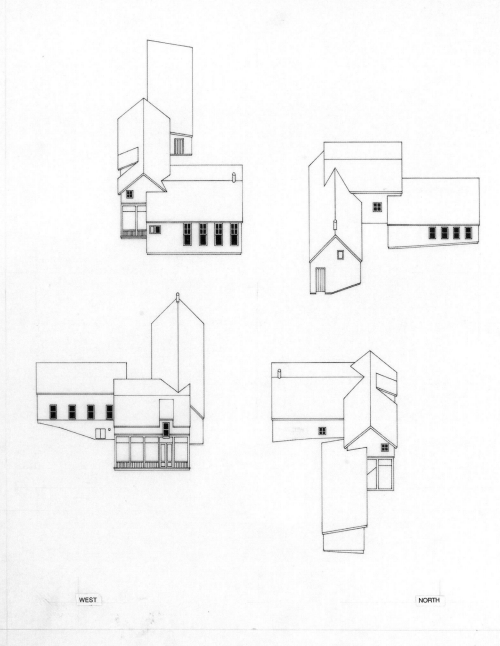

Nestled into a gentle slope, the guesthouse (left) and screened porch (right) are a play of complements and contrasts. The guesthouse rests on a masonry base and is clad in vertical board. The siding's orientation is reiterated in the tall legs of the porch's white frame, the horizontal elements of which, in turn, contrast with this volume's shingling.

Wide glass doors open from the central corridor into the screened porch; the studio's barn-type sliding door makes seclusion possible.

A steep set of stairs leads from a foyer off the guesthouse to the small room above the porch.

The James

Chicago, Illinois
2006

Located on Chicago's Near North Side, The James is operated by a company that is developing a line of hotels meant to appeal to the urban traveler with a taste for good design and stylish, up-to-the-minute amenities. Berke completely renovated the seventeen-story hotel that previously inhabited the building, reconfiguring the lobby and registration area and reducing the existing 324 suites to 297 units of various types. DBPA also constructed new facilities: a restaurant and two bars on the first floor and, on the second floor, a 2,500-square-foot ballroom, meeting rooms, and a private club. A fitness center and spa are found in the basement.

Berke's principal moves were to relocate the hotel's entrance from the side of the building to the front, on busy East Ontario Street, and to open the first-floor façade by inserting floor-to-ceiling windows, radically transforming the building's relationship to the street. The reoriented entrance gives onto a new lobby that, with the adjoining bar and lounge, establishes a strong longitudinal axis and creates a 125-foot-long vista and social mixing space. The revolving door initiates a perpendicular axis, along which guests are drawn to the terminating elevator lobby by a full-height mural of a birch forest.

The building, which was constructed in the 1920s, is U-shaped and organized around a light court. Berke filled in this court at the second story to create the ballroom, and added meeting spaces and a private club. Reorganization of the fifteen guest floors consisted largely of moving or removing interior walls to produce a mix of traditional king-size or double rooms, studios, lofts, and one-bedroom apartments, together with two penthouse units. This reshuffling also created alcoves for dining, working, or simply relaxing—a differentiation of spaces that imparts a residential quality to accommodations at The James. Throughout the hotel, finishes and furnishings are elegant but unpretentious, coalescing into architectural microclimates in each zone of the hotel. Custom-designed light fixtures and furniture, as well as commissioned works of art, complete The James's comfortably chic mise-en-scène.

View of front. By relocating the hotel's entrance and introducing considerable transparency in the ground-floor elevation, Berke created the opportunity for reciprocal spectacles: passersby witness the goings-on in the hotel lobby, while guests take in the liveliness of the street.

Opposite: Hotel lobby, with registration area at right and bar and lounge at rear. Terrazzo floors and columns clad in zinc and frosted mirrors establish a cool setting and, with their reflective qualities, magnify the natural illumination. A line of leather-covered lounge chairs forms one edge of a conversation area that is loosely organized into more intimate individual spaces defined by alcoves at the exterior wall.

Registration desk. Cool zinc and terrazzo contrast with warm plain-sawn hickory. The joints between sheets of zinc establish a datum that carries across the registration desk and throughout the lobby.

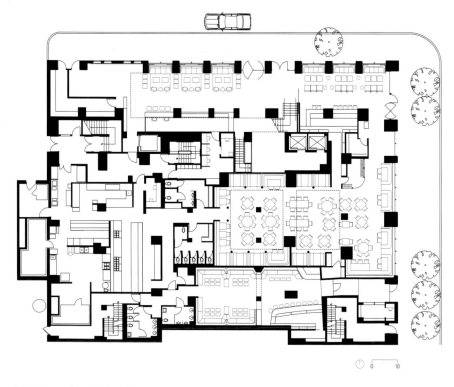

First-floor plan. Facing East Ontario Street along the front (north) of the hotel, the registration area and bar and lounge are the hub of public activity. The hotel also houses a more intimate restaurant and, at the rear of the building (south), a nightclub.

The library in the private James Club features walls clad in teak panels and custom-made chairs with chrome frames and ponyhair upholstery. The rear walls of the bookcases are hand-screened.

Opposite: Primehouse restaurant. A warm materials palette of oxidized bronze wall panels, chocolate-colored leather upholstery, and end-grain plywood floors imparts a mellow quality to the restaurant.

Above: Elevator lobby

Left: Loft guest room. A panel of dark-stained ash nearly the size of the wall is the backdrop for a platform bed of the same wood. The sleeping space is screened from the sitting room by a curtain of nickel-plated steel beads. Berke collaborated with Isometrix Lighting + Design Ltd on the creation of the lighting fixture.

Above: Penthouse. The variety of warm woods imbues the living area with the quality of a retreat from the bustle of the city beyond its windows.

Opposite: King-size guest room. A walnut pocket door separates the bedroom and bath from the living and dining areas.

Food & Shelter: Urban Farming and Affordable Homes

New Housing New York
Design Ideas Competition
Queens, New York
2004

The New Housing New York Design Ideas competition was initiated in 2004 by the New York City Council, AIA New York Chapter, and the City University of New York to stimulate fresh thinking about the seemingly intractable challenge of providing affordable, sustainable housing in New York City. From the three parcels identified by the organizers as typical future development opportunities, Berke selected an eleven-acre brownfield site on the waterfront in Astoria, Queens.

The firm's award-winning submission, titled Food & Shelter, proposed revitalization of the site through an environmentally sustainable mix of light industry, retail, affordable housing, and urban farms. Farm plots and low-rise apartment buildings alternate in a terraced landscape that steps up the site as it approaches the waterfront, culminating in a series of mid-rise towers with views west to Manhattan and back to Queens. A continuous boardwalk along the water's edge tethers the site to the larger Astoria neighborhood, and the site's interior streets continue as piers into the East River to capture the relationship of the neighborhood to the water.

Food & Shelter treats the apartment buildings as vertical counterparts to the farm plots. Deep two-story balconies on the south elevation of each structure are sandwiched within a double skin that traps warm air in the winter and provides appropriate conditions for container gardening in the summer. DBPA's scheme thus takes advantage of its site to offer views and access to the water; more significant, it fundamentally alters the landscape and the way in which one relates to and experiences it.

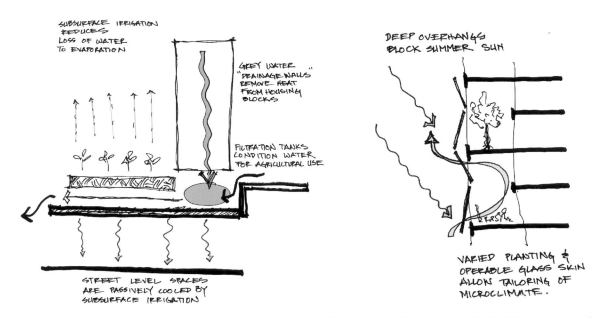

Left: Recycled gray water is used for the urban gardens and allows for passive cooling, minimizing the buildings' impact on the environment. Right: Concept for the louvered, double-skin façade

The exterior layer of the buildings' double skin façades is composed of large, operable glass louvers that permit tenants to control their environment and transform the elevation into a mosaic. The double-height balcony between this exterior layer and the fixed interior skin is deep enough to allow for planting, such that the façade is literally and figuratively "green."

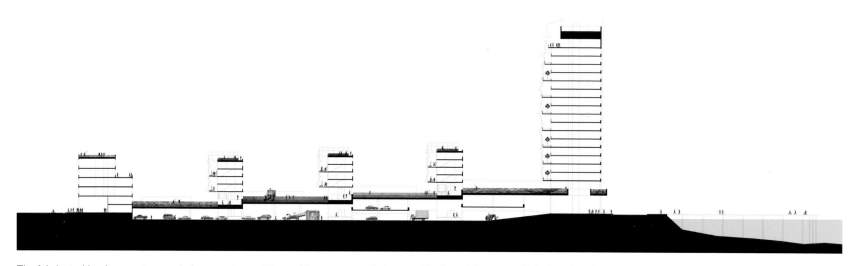

The fabricated landscape steps up in increments, and the parking garage roofs become the foundations on which the urban farms are planted.

The street wall and the buildings across the street define the site's southern edge and form the view corridor toward Manhattan.

Massing concept with urban farms planted on parking garage roofs

Row 1

...iba
...means to exploring the relationship ...smooth uniform surfaces (see ...ft.) and the prickly armatures that ...en (see thicket) ashiba, literally ...or a space wrapped in scaffolding ...n a wrapper (in America we say ...ntains, tents, clothing, etc. ashiba ...mple, a halfpipe may be ashiba.

Low
boards are seen in action: in the air, or in a blur, a low display offers the point of view in which most products will be seen on the mountain. product may be pulled out of the "drift" and checked out on the rumpled surface.

Clip
a flexible means of providing signage and other information.

Stencil
a less flexible but more rugged form of signage.

Jack-wall
the jack-wall is a user-operated interface with Burton where video clips, MP3 downloads, are exchanged. users may upload video clips of favorite runs for Burton review and possible projection. (see projection, realtime)

Row 2

...gout
...space should have ample space

Blur

blur is the tendency of objects to thin out into a long streaking form when registered at great speed or over long intervals of time. some fixtures within the Burton environment might have just this long, thin hyper-attenuated effect. (see speed rail)

Prolog
this is a tabulation of psychological, physiological, and physical effects that may be found in the Burton retail environment. in general, an attempt has been made to pare each down to its essential aspect so any can be combined and many discarded until the resultant proposal synthesizes a few of the most important sensations from the Rider experience.

our goal will be to choose those that combine best, and translate into a simple, versatile, and buildable proposition.

in general, ideas will be favored for their ability to offer a glimpse into Rider culture, or better, a brief actual sensation drawn from Riding. many ideas will actually serve two purposes: that brief sensation, and also to permit an easy simile for the novice. for example, an assemblage might perform a double-duty: on one hand speaking to the Rider "this you know," while permitting the uninitiated the realization "oh, so that's kind of like snow."

thus, in no particular order:

Mountain
the Burton environment, here modified away from its loner tendencies (like 'the old man of the mountain') toward a more 'social' form. a Burton space might promote a 'mountain mentality' in that it should be seen as an opportunity to try out the Rider experience.
the mountain can only be seen, objectified, from a distance, but on the mountain it is pieced together into a collage of sensations.

Row 3

...jection
...and information media will be ...onto surfaces and into thin air. ...and flicker)

Between
the boarder mentality finds space to carve everywhere. 'between' is a way to acknowledge the ambivalent 'in-between-ness' of many Rider activities: between high and low tech, between mountain and handrail, between accepted and outlawed. 'between' is also a way to exploit small residual spaces, the secret spaces left over by bigger things.

Thicket
some materials and assemblies will be chosen for their porosity and low shadow-density. the thicket might be an assemblage of wire crates and boxes capable of merchandising a variety of things. thicket will also be seen as an opportunity for flicker. thicket permits a loose simile to scrub brush, coniferous trees, and shrub edges.
thicket is a semi-transparent wall, like a stone wall (see mountain) made permeable. (see flicker)

Merch-drift
a super-thickened drift, a seat, a place for merchandise, a different kind of table or bench.

Row 4

...t wall
...all is an ashiba wall, a soft wall ...membrane in tension with hard ...nings (including some zippered ...hat you reach into.

...Is
...display cells that are partially ...in walls, allow non-soft walls ...ashiba, pods are another way to ...nse perimeter leaving the sense ...is clear for activity.

Datum
a horizon, a line that is held throughout the store against which various things (like the speed rail, or a series of similar fixtures for holding a variety of things), or any changing thing, are read. the datum is a line against which the experience is registered against.

Tate/Anti-Tate
at London's Tate gallery, portraits and other genres are grouped together regardless of period, instead of by their respective eras. in the Burton space, similar items for a given activity (all-weather clothing, gear, and a board for rugged conditions) could be displayed together.
alternately, Burton could pursue "anti-Tate" thinking, the extreme juxtaposition of unlike things is an alternative mentality of rider culture. (see high-lo-tech and between.) here, completely different categories of stuff could be displayed side-by-side on a single surface.

Materials
the Burton environment should emphasize neutral and authentic materials as a means to allowing the Burton products to grab the foreground.

Seamless
ultimately the Burton environment should be characterized by a forward-thinking high-tech approach to construction. the Burton space should be no less technologically advanced and innovative than the Burton products. the space may be deliberate in when and where it recedes into the background to showcase Burton products, but it should be nonetheless intelligently expressive of Burton.

Row 5

...t
...rumple, like earth, stairs, or

...-Object
...space might benefit from an ...' thinking that attempts to ...ost architectural moves within ...meter: within thick walls and ...e cash-wrap and stock areas ...handled this way in favor of open ...umbered floors. (see between,

Color
the Burton environment should emphasize natural colors, colors that are inherent to the materials that possess them, durable colors, and whites. the occasional burst of bright color should be deployed in a way that allows it to be easily changed from time to time. the chromatic mission of the Burton environment should be to allow the merchandise to stand out.

Hi-Lo-Tech
Riders are rugged can-do mountain types, who are nonetheless crazy about technology and high-tech stuff.

Speed Rail
allows you to clip into any part of the rail. densely merchandisable. offers opportunity for displaying merchandise as they would be seen on the slopes: up in the air, below, similes to speed. some fixtures can be merchandised with anything, some fixtures can literally sell anything. day-to-day flexibility and season-to-season changeability will characterize Burton stores.

Row 6

...tlety
...gestures proposed here should ...within a careful synthesis that ...space to feel whole and complete. ...coordinating these sensations ...ained but ultimately seamless ...it will be sought, again to give the ...ducts the greatest prominence.

Incline
a fundamental proposition here is that Riding exploits the deviation from the horizontal. floor surfaces may incline in the Burton retail space. walls may be pulled out of verticality by the gravity exerted by non-horizontal floors.

Rumple
a form of incline, a rich 3-d version composed of many small inclines. rumple permits a simile to snow and terrain, and is exalted here for its ability to project innovation and difference from convention. video images should be projected on rumple.
one favored context for merchandise should be a rumple-surface. (see low)

Air
another context for the display of boards and other merchandise is the sky. you should be able to see some boards, boots, bindings, etc. against the crisp cerulean of the sky. (see speed rail)

Row 7

...-Ashiba
...of ashiba. (imagine being in ...thicket.) are those in-between ...are dark spaces, useful spaces, ...spaces. between the domes of ...churches. (see between) these ...handbag, or they may be spaces ...to other activities (see changing

Delay/Repetition
the Burton environment might exploit the curious way in which many sports compete in pulses: head-to-head competition modified by delay (think of start-times)...

Flicker
the Burton environment may feature that light that characterizes riding: flickering light glinting through specular surfaces, coming in low, filtered by trees and scrub, (see thicket) and modulated at extreme speed. (see blur) flicker permits a loose simile to sunlight.

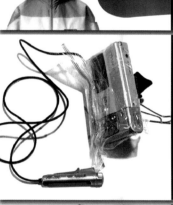

S-Form
a spatial realization of rumple, the Burton retail environment might reject the rectangular in favor of a richer, more complex, and sinuous space. similes to carving, similes to the natural environment.

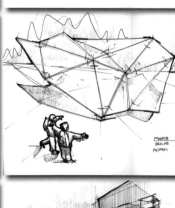

The Sum of the Parts

The Sum of the Parts

The elevator door opens onto the Howell Studio in New York City, and one is immersed in an environment of extraordinary calm. A loft of minimally articulated spaces, it is rendered in a light palette of materials and furnishings, relieved here by a metal picture rail, there by a marble countertop, the whole infused with an even, softly glowing light. A little over a mile to the southeast, Burton Snowboards SoHo buzzes with a palpable energy, expressed architecturally through a profusion of natural and man-made materials that complement the colorful products on display and resonate with the store's high-spirited human activity. At the 21c Museum Hotel in Louisville, Kentucky, initial absorption in the alternately challenging, amusing, and droll art on view gives way to awed discovery of a massive steel structure in the atrium gallery that hugs a brick wall like a girdle, as if to prevent it from falling into the gallery.

Diverse in character and function, these projects have in common a coalescence of composition, details, and materials that produces a seamless, coherent whole, appropriate and *specific* to the building's local conditions. While this synergy presumably is the objective of every architect, Berke's oeuvre is distinguished by the seeming effortlessness with which she achieves it. Almost unfailingly characterized by balance, composure, and a quality of naturalness, her work is marked by the absence of cunning or any sense that she has strained to assemble the elements of composition and detail into a totality. Berke's explanation of how she hopes these aspects of the work are experienced is characteristically nuanced:

> I don't really want people to *immediately* notice my details. If they notice the details right away, they're too virtuosic, too overtly crafted. I want details to be something you notice sort of on your third or fourth time, or that you *only* notice if you're deliberately looking. And I only want people to notice the composition subliminally. I would say that many, many, many of our details are not in the service of detail, but they're actually in service of composition. I think most of my details kind of go away a little bit, and the idea is that you see the greater composition. Is that true? Does that hold up?

Berke's questions pose something of a dilemma for the writer. On the one hand, drawing attention to composition and detail by dissecting Berke's work in terms of these elements undermines the assertion of their unity. On the other hand, to suggest that one can comprehend or experience a building or a space (regardless of who designed it) without taking note of any of these elements is like saying that it is

Above: Burton Snowboards, Burlington, Vermont, 2003. Tall wooden slat-walls and movable display furniture are two devices Berke designed to organize the retail space.

Opposite: 21c Museum Hotel, Louisville, Kentucky, 2002–6. Atrium gallery

48 Bond Street, New York, New York, 2006–8. An irregular arrangement of canted bay windows projects from the façade of flamed charcoal-gray granite. From a distance (see page 16), the façade reads as a unified whole; it is only at a closer perspective that the canted windows come into focus.

Face-vase figure-ground image illustrating the Gestalt theory of perception

possible to look at a person's face without registering its individual features. While one might take in a whole in the first moment of perception, the brain almost instantly begins to deconstruct the whole into its components.

How to unravel this analytical knot? Gestalt theory provides an appropriate context within which to consider the way architectural elements come together to form a whole in Berke's work. The figure-ground principle of Gestalt psychology, famously illustrated by the black-and-white image that reads alternately as two faces or a vase, holds that figure and ground can be perceived only in relation to each other, through their contrast. Each of these parts is in itself a whole, but the image they collectively constitute is initially recognized as another whole, rather than in its parts. Perception, in other words, shifts between part and whole. Although the popular adage that sums up this phenomenon is that the whole of an image (for example) is greater than the sum of its parts, the actual statement made by Wolfgang Köhler, one of the originators of Gestalt psychology, was that the whole is *different* from the sum of its parts. This proposition, according to one scholar, suggests that the *meaning* of the whole derives from something *outside* itself. The principle of extended wholes accounts for this: "In order to derive meaning and knowledge from contrast, we need at least one more dimension than any single part-whole context alone provides. This dimension lies within the extended whole or expanding context, and allows human perception to become meaningful knowledge."[1]

Thinking in terms of Gestalt theory about the way Berke uses the tools of the architect's trade—composition, materials, and details—to shape space and create form allows one to parse these elements without doing intellectual violence to the whole that she so smoothly creates. While their relative weight—their function, one might say, as figure versus ground—varies among the diverse projects represented in this section, the line of inquiry is not simply about individual gestures or design decisions, but about the experience engendered by the totality they constitute.

Among Berke's most affecting projects are those that involve a dramatic sectional intervention, creating unexpected views and peripheral spatial experiences. The 21c Museum Hotel, an amalgam pairing a boutique hotel with galleries for the display of contemporary art, was fashioned from five nineteenth-century brick warehouses. To create a dramatic two-story gallery within the four buildings that are contiguous with each other, Berke carved out the lower part of the walls in

21c Museum Hotel. Volume above the atrium gallery

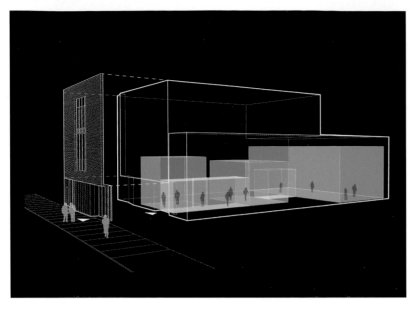

Marianne Boesky Gallery, New York, New York, 2004–7. The diagram reveals the sequence of volumes that comprise the building and generate its spatial complexity.

the two eastern buildings, inserting a steel truss system to reinforce the remaining structure. The volume above the gallery, punched with openings to admit light from the skylights into interior rooms, is visible from the gallery through the crossbeams of the trusses. One's experience of the lower gallery entails simultaneously the sublime and the accidentally voyeuristic: the reinforcing structure's scale and function are slightly terrifying, but this is relieved somewhat by the possibility of catching a glimpse of guests in the rooms above. Materials offer a different kind of contrast: between the sleek, smooth regularity of white plaster, for instance, and the more organic, variegated quality of end-grain flooring and the recycled poplar from which the plenum and reception desk were constructed. The whole reads as a careful balance, programmatically, materially, and perceptually.

Where the 21c Museum Hotel is the product of a surgically precise process of subtraction and insertion, the Marianne Boesky Gallery, an art gallery recently constructed in the Chelsea neighborhood of Manhattan, is an essay in the elaboration of space through sectional shaping. The building's location adjacent to a disused elevated railroad bed now being converted into a public park required that the building step back above the height of the tracks. Berke's response is a structure composed of a white brick box that is inserted into, but appears to be extruded from, a slightly larger metal and cinderblock base. This seemingly straightforward composition belies a much more complex section of two and a half stories. The resulting interior organization is a collection of volumes of various dimensions that are experienced as a sequence of changing degrees of expansion and compression and, in some cases, offer tantalizing sidelong glimpses from one space to another. The asymmetrical composition enabled the insertion of light funnels over the larger of the two galleries, transforming the space into a microcosmic reflection of the changing exterior environment.

Berke's use of different materials to articulate the volumes of the Marianne Boesky Gallery lends the building a tactile draw that it shares with a house she designed in Fort Lauderdale. The Sospiro

Plane Space Gallery, New York, New York, 2001–2. Although considerably smaller than the Marianne Boesky Gallery, this 1,200-square-foot space has in common with it an asymmetry of plan and movement. To effect the conversion of a nineteenth-century firehouse into a flexible venue for art exhibitions, Berke inserted sliding walls that can be arranged to create one large area or up to three distinct rooms. As in the Boesky Gallery, illumination—here, lighting coves carved into the walls and ceilings—plays an important role in one's experience of the space.

Opposite: Marianne Boesky Gallery. South façade

Sospiro Canal House, Fort Lauderdale, Florida, 2001–4. The swimming-pool court is anchored by the wood volume that contains a guest room and an office.

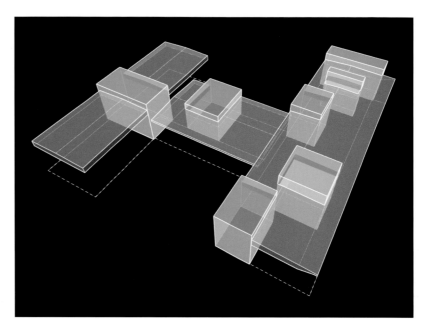

Sospiro Canal House. Diagram showing programmatic organization

Canal House is an assemblage of programmatic boxes organized into a plan that takes the rough form of an "I"; its exterior is clad in rich mahogany and sensuous Keys stone. Using a strategy similar to that at the Boesky Gallery, Berke called out the boxes by dressing them in stone, throwing them into visual relief against the elements articulated in mahogany. In several cases, the box is pulled slightly through its perimeter wall, creating a literal sense of sculptural relief. The compositional push-pull makes the house legible from the outside and shapes the flow of interior space into a path that wends its way between and around the programmatic elements. Where the mahogany acts on the exterior as a visually recessive foil to the Keys stone, on the interior it engages in a somewhat unexpected harmony with blonde wood floors, white plaster walls, and a vibrant red kitchen to create a great sense of warmth.

The way in which metal and brick, Keys stone and wood express relationships among parts in these two projects reflects Berke's sensitivity to what I will call the narrative capacity of materials. This is a nuanced twist on the old chestnut about the expressive potential of materials, which attributes emotive qualities to materials. In the work of Rudolph Schindler, for example, this potential is manifested as a kind of sculptural quality, rather than suggesting anything about how the building functions or what it says about its users. By narrative capacity of materials, I mean their ability to reveal something about a building's underlying ideas and aspirations, whether at the level of its overall organization or in terms of the articulation of its interior. Like a literary text, a building might embody multiple, even contradictory, material narratives. In relation to the Marianne Boesky Gallery and the Sospiro Canal House, the notion refers to the impression that exterior materials divulge the organization of the structure by differentiating its components. At the Boesky Gallery, it turns out, the impression is deceptive, as the building is more complex spatially than its composition of simple boxes would suggest. At the Sospiro Canal House, the alternations in exterior materials that reflect discrete moves along the programmatic path tell only part of the story. In some places in the house, the system of mahogany siding and window framing blurs the reading of the rooms from the exterior, infuses complexity into the window rhythm, and, where the framing turns a corner, erodes planar continuity.

At the more intimate scale of an interior, the narrative function of materials is related to the client's image of herself or himself. It is a truism that the decisions made by an architect and client collectively constitute a statement of the client's design identity. What sets Berke's work apart in this regard are her subversions of what might be considered the semantic or connotative characteristics of materials. In her hands, unremarkable materials acquire a subtle elegance, while even the most luxurious materials can project a quality of self-effacement. In the guest rooms at the 21c Museum Hotel, repurposed polypropylene is used to make headboards on which limited-edition prints are tacked up for guests to take home. If, by contrast, walls of vellum or closets sheathed in leather would seem to be conspicuous marks of status, in Berke's hands they become restrained bearers of the domestic conviviality radiated by the owners of a loft in New York City. The vellum also plays a part in the articulation of form and space. The walls that are clad in it define a structure that literally contains the kitchen, isolating it within the large living/dining area. The kitchen volume, in turn, is slightly offset from the line defining one side of the long, principal corridor, subtly altering one's perspectival experience of the corridor. Although the vellum box is not the physical center of the loft, it is, in effect, the anchor of the composition, demarcating the point at which open, public spaces give way to the private domain. The material thus both imparts a message about the clients' elegant taste and acts as a point of orientation.

21c Museum Hotel. Polypropylene headboard

Where details are important carriers of meaning in the residences described above, they constitute the totality of Berke's design for a system of fixtures for the display of merchandise in Calvin Klein's cK line of stores. (The stores, which were established worldwide in the 1990s as both freestanding retailers and department-store boutiques, are no longer in existence.) The DNA of Berke's system was a collection of simple units—brackets, shelves, rods, hooks, cubbies, table bases, and tabletops fabricated in hot-rolled steel, wood, and glass— that could be arranged in countless permutations for adaptation to any site. The "architecture" of the cK interior was the aggregation of these arrangements and the spatial sequences defined or implied by their layouts. In the cK system, the whole *was* the parts.

What of Berke's questions? Does detail serve composition? Is composition in effect invisible? There is a certain paradox in the fact that the close study of the work entailed in responding to these queries makes impossible the innocent experience of Berke's architecture that her subtly complex analysis implies. Perhaps the questions are simply her way of prodding users—and herself—to contemplate the sources of architectural satisfaction. Despite their varied scale, typology, and approach to making form, the projects in this section highlight the agility and flexibility with which Berke consistently brings together composition, materials, and detail to create an experience that is greater than the sum of these constituent parts.

NOTE
1. A. Manja Larcher, "The Origin of Meaning: Gestalt in a Reconsidered Context," *AABSS Perspectives* (electronic journal of the American Association of Behavioral and Social Sciences), http://aabss.org/journal2003/Larcher.htm.

Liberty Street Loft, New York, New York, 2003–5. Wall of vellum "box" that wraps the kitchen

21c Museum Hotel

Louisville, Kentucky
2002–6

This unusual hybrid comprises a 6,000-square-foot art museum, a ninety-one-room full-service boutique hotel, and a world-class restaurant. Berke's reconceptualization of five nineteenth-century tobacco and bourbon warehouses that are listed on the National Register of Historic Places fulfilled the developers' objectives of making their substantial collection of contemporary art accessible to the public while preserving the buildings through adaptive reuse. A destination almost immediately upon its opening, 21c (meaning twenty-first-century) also has advanced the revitalization of downtown Louisville.

In order to retain as much of the existing structures as possible while permitting the new hotel rooms to have windows, Berke carved out a void at the heart of the group of joined buildings.

By strategically punching openings in the existing party walls, she transformed the void into an atrium that admits natural light into the surrounding rooms. Through the glass floor of the atrium, light streams into a second, lower atrium, which contains expansive gallery space. In both spaces, the massive steel structure reinforcing the original brick walls is visible.

21c's compositional and programmatic complexity is simultaneously amplified and modulated by a multi-textured palette of materials— brick, various woods, and concrete, among others—and thoughtful detailing. DBPA designed the interiors, retaining or repurposing original elements where possible and employing innovative and environmentally responsible materials. The result is a surprising coalescence of the historic and the contemporary, the comfortable and the cool, into a building that is both provocative and welcoming.

The museum and hotel combines five historic warehouses.

Metal-and-glass canopies on Seventh Street bring a subtle contemporary touch to the entrance of the finely textured brick exterior, yet allow the historic door surround to hold its weight. The roof of the smallest of the five buildings (at left) serves as outdoor space for the adjacent penthouse guest rooms.

The registration desk and soffit punctured with lights are made of poplar recycled from beams removed during construction of the atria. End-grain flooring, a ceiling of beadboard, and poplar form a palette of textures.

Berke flanked each existing cast-iron column in the upper gallery with new steel columns. The entrance to the lower, double-height gallery and a portion of the steel structure that supports it are visible beyond the trio of columns.

Berke inserted a thick "liner" in the upper gallery to create walls for art and to house HVAC systems without lowering the ceiling or inserting ceiling ducts. Original brick walls are visible above the liner, whose low height allows the eye to carry across the gallery and through to the restaurant beyond, lending the space a sense of continuity.

The cantilevered stairway to the lower gallery is constructed of steel and translucent glass. The handrail carved into the walls complements its metal counterpart on the other side of the stairway.

In the lower gallery, windows of interior hotel rooms are visible between beams of the steel structure (as at upper right).

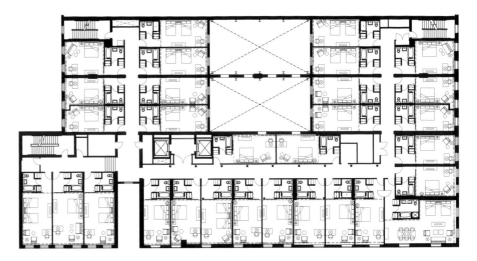

Plan of a typical guest-room floor

First-floor plan. The dashed lines within the atrium represent the wall reinforced by the steel structure to create the double-height gallery.

Basement plan

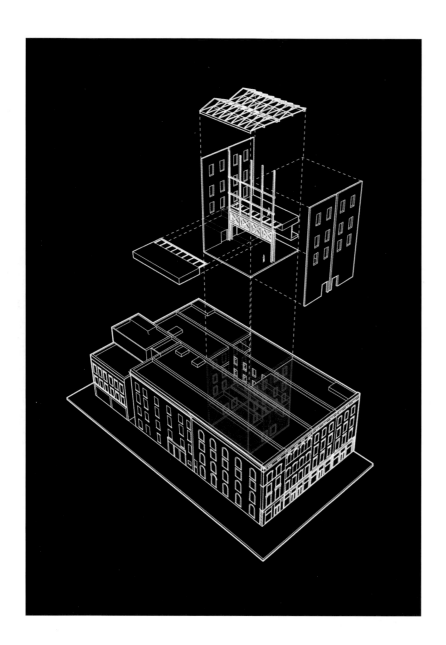

A concept drawing reveals the means by which DBPA inserted the new structure and fashioned the fenestrated void at the building's core.

Original brick walls were punctured with windowlike openings and reinforced by a steel frame to create the upper atrium that admits natural light for guest rooms. Berke retained some of the original wood beams.

At each elevator landing, art is displayed in full-height vitrines built out from the original brick walls.

Guest room. Among the furnishings Berke designed is the headboard, fitted out with a tackable surface on which works of art can be hung. She also designed the green/blue blankets, which were made by a local weaving group.

In the restaurant, Proof-on-Main, Berke deploys the same materials palette and thoughtful architectural insertions that are found elsewhere in the project.

Exterior view of restored façades

Marianne Boesky Gallery

New York, New York
2004–7

Located in Chelsea, the new 10,000-square-foot building for the Marianne Boesky Gallery features two floors of gallery, art preparation, and administration spaces, as well as a caretaker's apartment. Acknowledging the High Line, an abandoned elevated railroad that is the city's newest public greenway, the building volume sets back along the shared property line. This setback generated the structure's complex composition: a glazed-white-brick volume that is inserted asymmetrically into an L-shape of corrugated metal and flanked by a concrete-block mass. While these materials are at home among the old warehouses, garages, and elevated railroad that, at this writing, still give the neighborhood its industrial charac-

ter, they also convey a contemporary and subtly refined character. The brick is an updated, more elegantly finished version of standard brick, while the concrete block, with its custom blend of aggregate, has a smooth, ground face that lends subtle nuance to this inexpensive material.

Berke arranged the gallery's interior spaces in a sequence that creates a rich experience of discovery. From the front door, a generous entry hall leads past the reception area and a private viewing room to a gallery. Beyond, the building opens up to a second, larger gallery measuring 28 by 56 feet. The three broad light monitors that puncture its eighteen-foot ceiling provide unexpected glimpses of the sky and the rare opportunity to view art in an environment of subtly changing natural light.

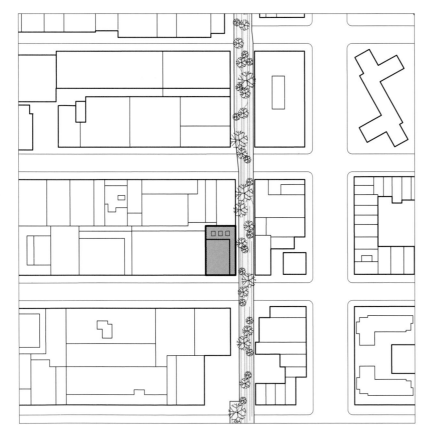

The immediate architectural setting of the Marianne Boesky Gallery is a rich mix of scales—buildings with large footprints to the west and smaller structures to the east—which is mediated by Berke's assemblage of boxes. The elevated High Line runs north-south immediately to the east of the building.

View from the entrance. Berke's elegant but neutral palette allows the architecture to register in one's consciousness without overwhelming the art. A series of brushed-steel panels opposite the receptionist's desk (at right) functions both to reveal and conceal. The left-most panel is a pocket door that opens onto the project room, while the conventional hinged door at the far right gives onto back-of-house areas. The vista down the corridor terminates at a wall of the first, small gallery but also reveals a bit of the larger gallery beyond.

Project room. Throughout the building, hard-troweled concrete floors and plaster walls provide a neutral backdrop for the display of art.

Large gallery, with ceiling punctured by light monitors

View from the entrance corridor toward West 24th Street. The project room is at right.

An unusual amount of natural light reaches administrative offices through skylights that are made possible by the setback along the High Line.

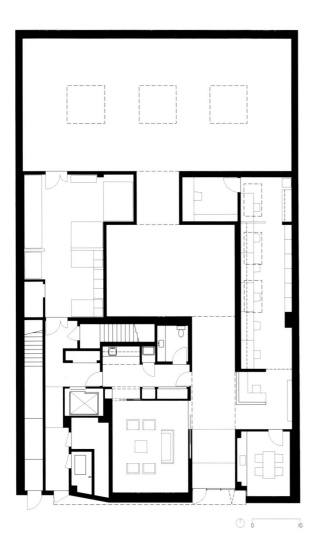

First-floor plan

122

Project room. The triple-height window in the front elevation is expressed at the street level as a clerestory.

The brick-clad mass projects slightly beyond the L-shaped volume, providing cover at the entrances to the building and imparting scale and relief to the street face. Berke gently canted the wall of corrugated metal as it approaches the door at the left to give the brick volume greater definition.

Howell Studio

New York, New York
1996–97

The open plan and aesthetic qualities that have come to define the classic New York City loft were refined by Berke through a precisely orchestrated set of moves in creating this combination painting studio, exhibition space, and residence for a painter and his wife. Occupying the entire floor of a cast-concrete building that was erected in 1909 and originally housed horse stables, the Howell Studio rejoins two long units that resulted from an earlier renovation. Although the solid masses housing the elevator, emergency stair, and a chimney block might have become design constraints, DBPA exploited them as devices for organizing program and circulation. The architects expanded the elevator/stair structure to create a core that, with the longitudinal axis marking the juncture of the two original units, defines the hub around which living, working, and exhibition spaces are composed. The owners' use of the loft flows naturally around these islands in an unimpeded, neatly composed manner.

The resoluteness of the plan is complemented by an extraordinarily subtle manipulation of the space-forming qualities of color, light, and materials. Because the artist's work is an ongoing exploration of extremely fine gradations of the color gray, the clients desired a neutral environment that would not distract the artist or compete with

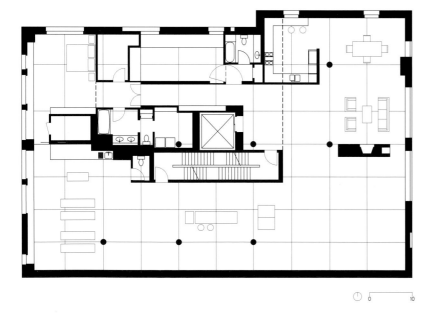

Residential areas are concentrated on one side of the loft, while studio and exhibition space occupy the other. Saw-cut control joints in the concrete floor give the plan its modular regularity.

his paintings. To create what appears to be completely consistent color throughout the loft, DBPA painted walls, ceilings, and other elements in slightly varying tones of white. In addition, lighting fixtures are arranged and natural illumination controlled to maintain even lighting. Wherever possible, vertical surfaces are uninterrupted and joints concealed, further enhancing spatial coherence. Saw cuts in the new, smooth concrete floor were carefully positioned to complement plan moves and underscore spatial alignments. The existing rough concrete-beam construction and mottled concrete floor impart texture to an otherwise serenely uniform environment, creating a tour de force of composition and detail.

View from living area toward studio/exhibition space

View from exhibition space toward living area. The two columns and the saw-cut joint that connects them define an implied boundary between the living/dining area and the kitchen, to its left. The joints in the concrete floor bring subtle Euclidean order to space that might otherwise feel somewhat centrifugal.

The exceptional consistency of the palette and the light filtering through translucent window shades creates an environment of surpassing tranquility.

126

Studio

Studio

Exhibition space

cK Calvin Klein

Worldwide
1995–99

In 1995, Berke won an invited competition held by Calvin Klein to create a design identity for its cK line of casual wear, jeans, cosmetics, eyewear, and underwear. DBPA designed a kit of parts—including standardized spatial configurations, furniture, fixtures, material finishes, lighting, display systems, signage, and video—that together create a complete retail environment. The governing idea of a flexible and universal system that could be adapted to the varying base building conditions of cK's network of boutiques and in-store showrooms was served by the development of a menu of components from which freestanding furniture and wall-mounted fixtures are constructed. Variously configured compositions of hooks, rods, brackets, shelves, cubbies, rails, bases, and tabletops fabri-

cated in a restrained material palette of hot-rolled steel, wood, and glass are carefully juxtaposed and presented against white walls.

The air of refined simplicity communicated by the cK system's elements is accentuated by a forthright attitude toward their assembly. Connections and joints between components are unabashedly revealed, resulting in a clear hierarchy of relationships: the floor and walls support steel brackets, steel supports wood and glass, and these finish materials support clothing. In turn, the arrangements of fixtures, furnishings, and walls define interlocking pods of space and chart varying paths through the store. Splashes of intense color simultaneously disrupt and reinforce the restraint of the palette, highlighting the fact that Berke's cK environment is fundamentally an accumulation of carefully considered details.

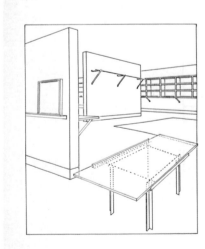

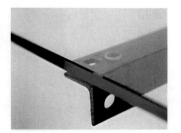

Page from Berke's original competition entry

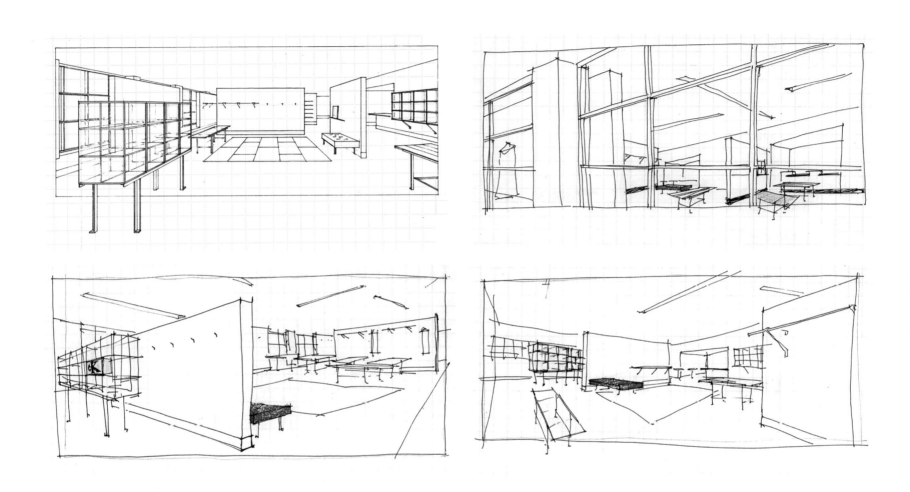

Early presentation sketches

cK Milan. Although the elements of Berke's kit of parts can be composed in any number of ways, an underlying order informs the system. In the Milan store, that order is complemented by the lucid articulation of the architecture.

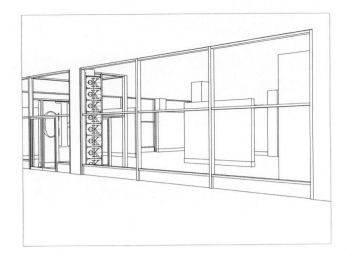

facade

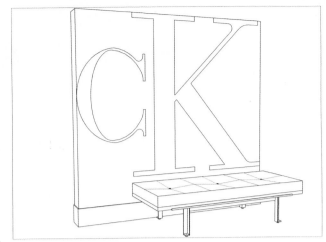

logo

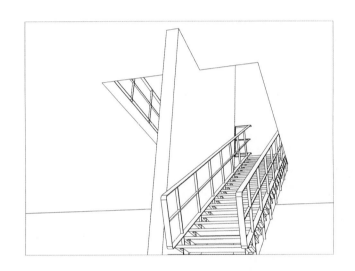

stair

fragrance

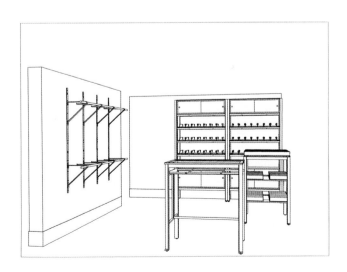

underwear

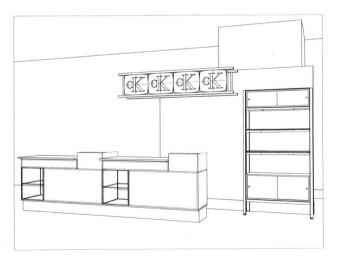

cash/ wrap

Architectural components of the cK branding strategy

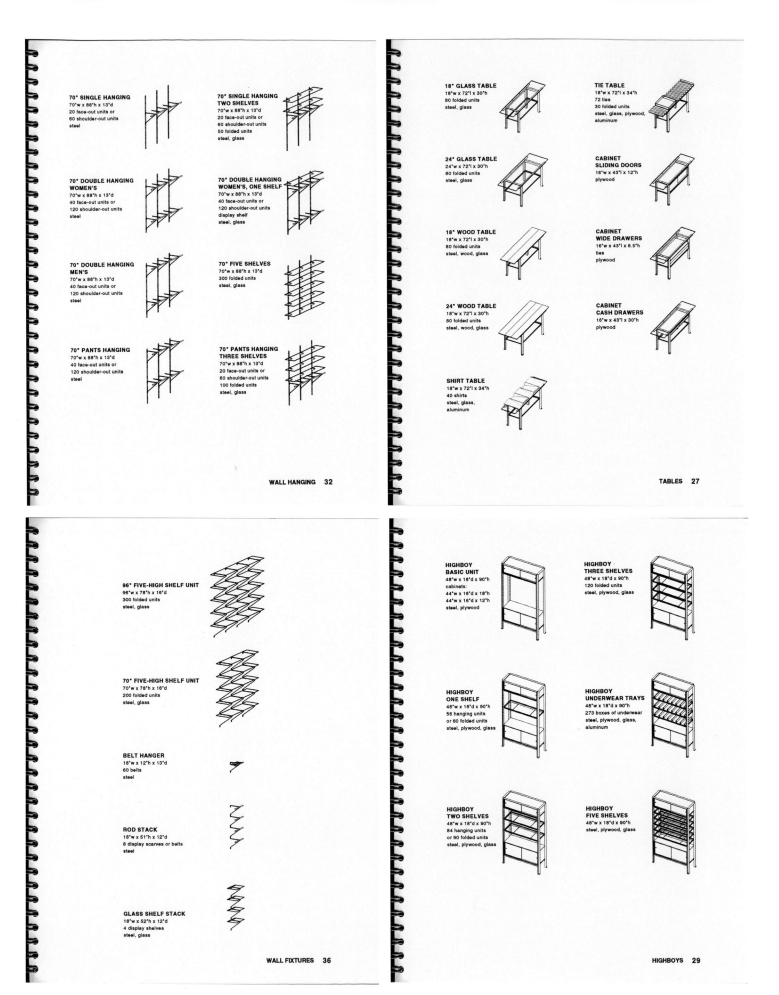

70" SINGLE HANGING
70"w x 88"h x 13"d
20 face-out units or
60 shoulder-out units
steel

70" SINGLE HANGING TWO SHELVES
70"w x 88"h x 13"d
20 face-out units or
60 shoulder-out units
50 folded units
steel, glass

70" DOUBLE HANGING WOMEN'S
70"w x 88"h x 13"d
40 face-out units or
120 shoulder-out units
steel

70" DOUBLE HANGING WOMEN'S, ONE SHELF
70"w x 88"h x 13"d
40 face-out units or
120 shoulder-out units
display shelf
steel, glass

70" DOUBLE HANGING MEN'S
70"w x 88"h x 13"d
40 face-out units or
120 shoulder-out units
steel

70" FIVE SHELVES
70"w x 88"h x 13"d
300 folded units
steel, glass

70" PANTS HANGING
70"w x 88"h x 13"d
40 face-out units or
120 shoulder-out units
steel

70" PANTS HANGING THREE SHELVES
70"w x 88"h x 13"d
20 face-out units or
60 shoulder-out units
100 folded units
steel, glass

WALL HANGING   32

18" GLASS TABLE
18"w x 72"l x 30"h
80 folded units
steel, glass

TIE TABLE
18"w x 72"l x 34"h
72 ties
30 folded units
steel, glass, plywood, aluminum

24" GLASS TABLE
24"w x 72"l x 30"h
80 folded units
steel, glass

CABINET SLIDING DOORS
16"w x 43"l x 12"h
plywood

18" WOOD TABLE
18"w x 72"l x 30"h
80 folded units
steel, wood, glass

CABINET WIDE DRAWERS
16"w x 43"l x 8.5"h
ties
plywood

24" WOOD TABLE
18"w x 72"l x 30"h
80 folded units
steel, wood, glass

CABINET CASH DRAWERS
16"w x 43"l x 30"h
plywood

SHIRT TABLE
18"w x 72"l x 34"h
40 shirts
steel, glass, aluminum

TABLES   27

96" FIVE-HIGH SHELF UNIT
96"w x 78"h x 16"d
300 folded units
steel, glass

70" FIVE-HIGH SHELF UNIT
70"w x 78"h x 16"d
200 folded units
steel, glass

BELT HANGER
18"w x 12"h x 13"d
60 belts
steel

ROD STACK
18"w x 51"h x 12"d
8 display scarves or belts
steel

GLASS SHELF STACK
18"w x 52"h x 12"d
4 display shelves
steel, glass

WALL FIXTURES   36

HIGHBOY BASIC UNIT
48"w x 18"d x 90"h
cabinets:
44"w x 16"d x 18"h
44"w x 16"d x 12"h
steel, plywood

HIGHBOY THREE SHELVES
48"w x 18"d x 90"h
120 folded units
steel, plywood, glass

HIGHBOY ONE SHELF
48"w x 18"d x 90"h
56 hanging units
or 60 folded units
steel, plywood, glass

HIGHBOY UNDERWEAR TRAYS
48"w x 18"d x 90"h
273 boxes of underwear
steel, plywood, glass, aluminum

HIGHBOY TWO SHELVES
48"w x 18"d x 90"h
84 hanging units
or 90 folded units
steel, plywood, glass

HIGHBOY FIVE SHELVES
48"w x 18"d x 90"h
steel, plywood, glass

HIGHBOYS   29

Fixtures and furnishings in Berke's final "Project Manual" illustrating the kit of parts

cK Milan

Liberty Street Loft

New York, New York
2003–5

This 5,200-square-foot loft faces Ground Zero in Lower Manhattan. Berke's renovation of the apartment synthesizes richly nuanced materials and discreet architectural moves to create a serene, contemplative space. The apartment's four exposures are carefully modulated to control light and views, contributing to the loft's spatial coherence.

Public and private zones are clearly distinguished in the T-shaped plan, with the living/dining area and kitchen occupying the large open volume that dominates its northern half. Berke enclosed the kitchen in a vellum-sheathed box, the long side of which defines the edge of the large living space. The sumptuous yet understated materials palette of the public areas—dark-stained rift-sawn oak floors, rubbed-plaster walls, and kitchen components of zebrawood, in addition to the vellum—elicits a variety of sensory experiences. New soundproof windows are encased in full-height "light boxes" that bring light to the ceiling and floor, further refining the environment.

The public spaces are connected to the apartment's private reaches by a wide corridor that is delineated by a strip of in-floor LED lights. Programmatic elements on the west side of the hallway were conceived as a sequence of solids that are perceived as objects, while the east side is presented as a continuous surface punctured by the doors of the rooms opening from it. The asymmetrical placement in the ceiling and floor of lights in two sizes complements this programmatic differentiation. The vellum box containing the kitchen is set slightly off the axis established by the sequence of solids, creating a telescoping perspective down the hallway that appears to exaggerate its length. One is initially struck by the richness of materials at the Liberty Street Loft, but ultimately it is these subtle gestures that capture sustained attention—and produce the double take for which Berke is known.

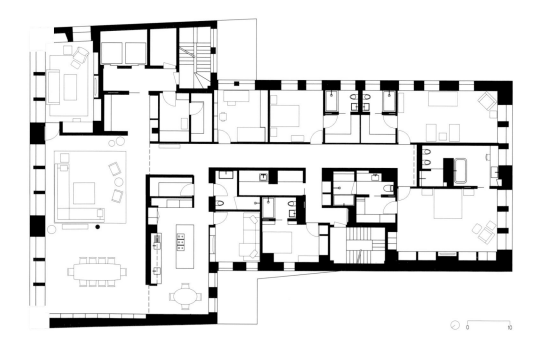

Leather-clad closet doors, silk rugs, and floor-to-ceiling windows are elements of the loft's common language.

The island defines the kitchen's work areas. Zebrawood cabinetry contrasts with the oak floors in both tonality and grain.

Living/dining area. At left is the vellum-sheathed box containing the kitchen.

Opposite: Corridor leading to the private realm. Plaster walls were left unpainted throughout the loft, giving them a lustrous quality. Because the beading of the wall joints is also unpainted, the walls read as distinct planes rather than as surfaces bending around a corner.

Sospiro Canal House

Fort Lauderdale, Florida
2001–4

The Sospiro Canal House occupies a gently sloping site along one of the city's intracoastal canals. Presenting a mute façade to the street and a more open, transparent elevation to the canal, the house is organized as a series of discrete programmatic "boxes" that are linked to form an I-shaped plan. Courtyards on either side of the house's central section, a breezeway between the house proper and the guest quarters, and a terrace facing the canal provide distinct and programmatically specific settings in which to experience the tropical landscape and climate.

Designed with an eye to the clients' desire for flexibility in displaying their extensive collection of contemporary art, the house's spatial configuration is alternately flowing and bounded, open and intimate. The center of activity—the informal dining area adjacent to the kitchen—is also the house's physical center. This space, which is reached from the front entrance via a hallway that steps down several feet to register a change in the site's elevation, is both a

Mahogany exterior walls and window grids recede beneath a deep stucco overhang that extends the length of the house, giving the impression that parts of the house are carved out of the Keys stone.

destination and the point from which the courtyards and public and private zones radiate. The defined path gives way at this juncture to more open circulation, and the distinction between interior and exterior is eroded by extensive fenestration in the spaces facing the courtyards and in the living/dining area, with its views of the canal.

In both composition and detail, the Sospiro Canal House is richly complex but legible. Although the house is 6,000 square feet, differ-

entiation of the programmatic elements as boxes clad or detailed in Keys stone and mahogany has the effect of diminishing its scale. A reduced palette of interior materials and finishes—relieved by the bright red kitchen cabinetry—and great subtlety in the treatment of lighting fixtures, mechanical ventilation grilles, and the like allow the art to comfortably inhabit the house without competition. Paying equally thoughtful attention to tectonic components, interiors, and exterior details, Berke creates a thoroughly cohesive and satisfying building.

Understated materials make a discreet but commanding impression from the moment one reaches the house. The elegantly taciturn front façade conceals volumes containing an office and guest room, an exercise room and storage, and, at right, a three-car garage.

Left: View from the canal side. Guest rooms occupy the stone-and-mahogany box at the near end of the house. The deep, canted overhang provides shade, minimizes solar gain, and allows the owners to limit their reliance on air-conditioning. The outbuilding at the far right is the boathouse.

Entry hall

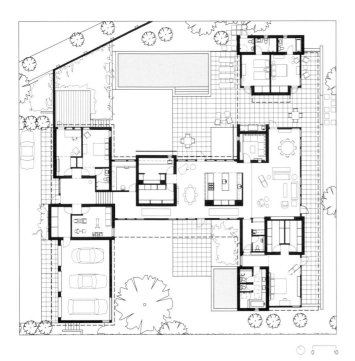

The wood-clad kitchen volume acts as an island around which one circulates from the informal dining space to other parts of the house.

Above: The informal dining area is the physical center of the house.

Opposite: Night view into the kitchen and informal dining area from the swimming-pool courtyard

In the living room and formal dining area, a grid of windows admits copious light and offers broad views of the canal.

View from the terrace toward the living/dining area. The guesthouse is at right.

The south terrace provides a quieter, more private alternative to the swimming-pool courtyard.

The master suite is the only part of the main house where the walls are not white. The bedroom, with furniture designed by Berke, opens onto the canal-side terrace.

An opening on the canal side of the building funnels breezes into the swimming-pool courtyard and acts as a buffer between the guesthouse (left) and the house proper.

Industria Superstudio

New York, New York
1990–91

Industria Superstudio rents studios, editing space, conference rooms, and casting facilities as well as backdrops, lights, and other equipment to fashion photographers on a daily basis; in the evenings, the complex serves as a premier event space. The adaptive reuse of this 20,000-square-foot, two-story building in Manhattan's West Village, an auto repair garage built in the 1930s, takes advantage of a column grid of approximately twenty-four feet on the ground floor and ninety-foot clear-span vaulted trusses on the second floor. The original automobile ramp from the street to the second floor is the primary circulation route and allows access for large props.

The client shared Berke's appreciation of the structure's rough industrial quality, and the renovation revealed its soaring spatial volumes. To achieve the architectural crispness and cleanness required by fashion photography, however, DBPA inserted a series of new flat white planes parallel and perpendicular to the grid and trusses, bringing tectonic and spatial legibility to the building. Berke also constructed cycloramas, which are permanent concrete-and-plaster versions of the photographer's traditional seamless backdrop.

Elements designed by Berke underscore and were inspired by the industrial character of the original structure. Among these were lighting assembled from stock industrial parts, overscale hinges and functional hardware, and a suite of custom furnishings, including a much-copied makeup table constructed of scaffolding sections.

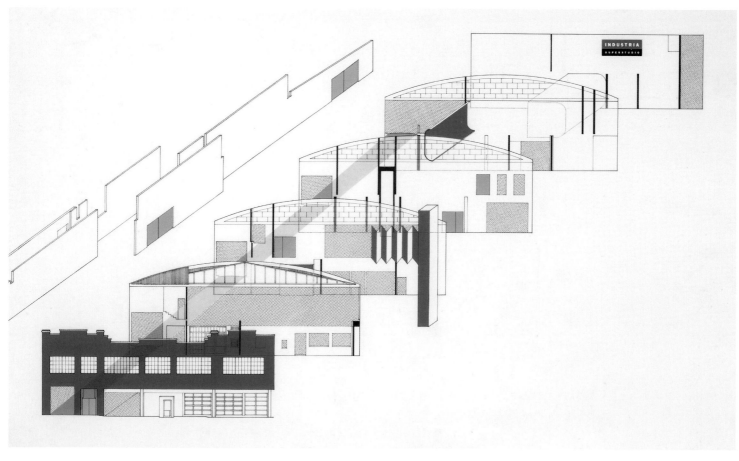

Parallel planes (shown receding along the automobile ramp, shaded in gray) and perpendicular planes (abstracted at the left of the drawing) were inserted to define studio, storage, and other support spaces.

Every change of level in the building is indicated by a steel staircase, and each of the five studios is marked by an asymmetrical pair of doors.

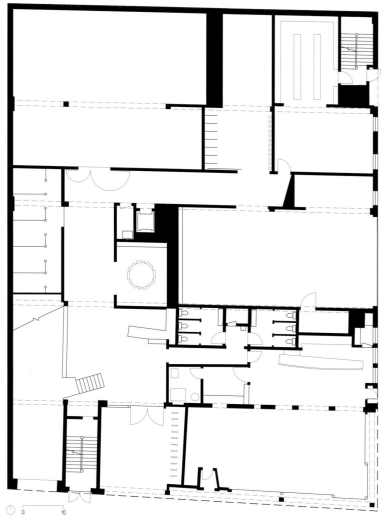

Industrial light fixtures, the rough concrete floor, and the retention of the building's cross-bracing evidence the client's and architect's admiration for the original qualities of the structure. The skylight was enlarged and rebuilt in the renovation.

First-floor plan

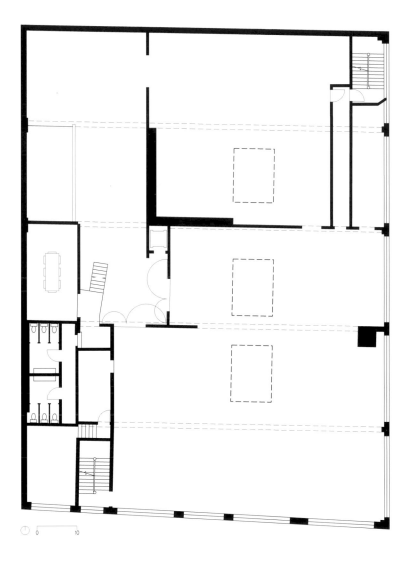

Second-floor plan

Berke preserved a wood lattice truss discovered in renovating the second floor. She created a clerestory by placing windows along the truss—the dominant feature of the largest studio. Furniture designed by Berke includes makeup tables and privacy screens.

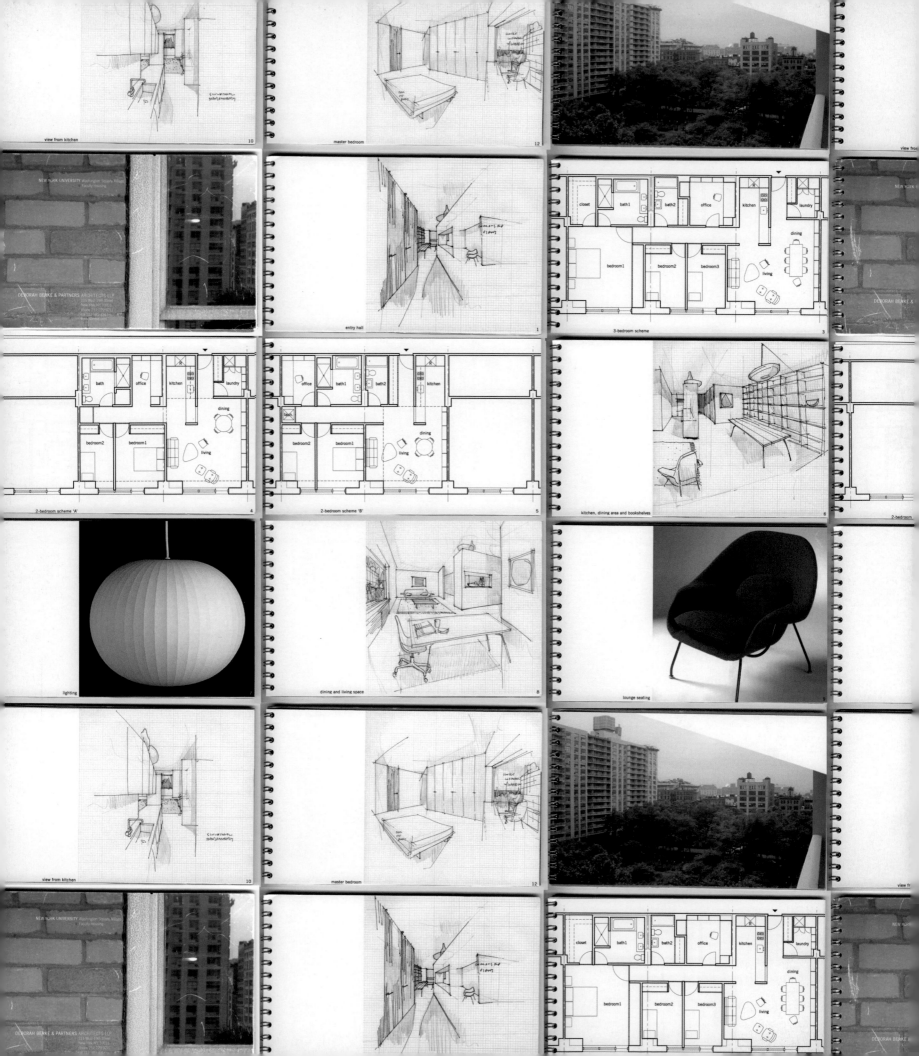

view from kitchen   10

master bedroom   12

view fro

NEW YORK UNIVERSITY Washington Square Village
Faculty Housing

DEBORAH BERKE & PARTNERS ARCHITECTS LLP
213 West 19th Street
New York, NY 10011
Phone 212.229.9211
Fax 212.229.4214

entry hall   1

| closet | bath1 | bath2 | office | kitchen | laundry |

bedroom1   bedroom2   bedroom3   living   dining

3-bedroom scheme   3

NEW YORK

DEBORAH BERKE &

| bath | office | kitchen | laundry |

bedroom2   bedroom1   living   dining

2-bedroom scheme 'A'   4

| office | bath1 | bath2 | kitchen |

bath

bedroom2   bedroom1   living   dining

2-bedroom scheme 'B'   5

kitchen, dining area and bookshelves   6

2-bedroom

lighting

dining and living space   8

lounge seating   9

view from kitchen   10

master bedroom   12

view fr

NEW YORK UNIVERSITY Washington Square Village
Faculty Housing

DEBORAH BERKE & PARTNERS ARCHITECTS LLP
213 West 19th Street
New York, NY 10011

NEW YOR

| closet | bath1 | bath2 | office | kitchen | laundry |

bedroom1   bedroom2   bedroom3   living   dining

DEBORAH BERKE &

Meaning in Architecture

Meaning in Architecture

In the first century B.C.E., the Roman architect, engineer, and theorist Marcus Vitruvius Pollio famously defined as the essential qualities of architecture *firmitas*, *utilitas*, and *venustas*, or, as commonly understood, firmness, commodity, and delight. The tidiness of this formulation both belies the complexities of making architecture and embodies its most intractable and fascinating challenge: the task of describing its effects. While *firmitas* (structural stability) and *utilitas* (suitability of a building to its purposes) are qualities that to some extent can be objectively assessed, *venustas*—which also can be rendered in English as loveliness, charm, attractiveness, or beauty— alludes to the necessarily subjective, often synaesthetic character of one's *experience* of a building. In a sense, the third term encompasses the first two and is the product of them. What is missing from this familiar triad but is implied by it is some accounting for the production of architectural meaning, which ultimately is created through the use of—through an active engagement with—a building or place. It is within this context that the full measure of Deborah Berke's work can be taken. The projects in the following section, the majority of which are workspaces, exemplify ways in which architectural meaning emerges as a result of use.

To say that architecture acquires its meaning through use is to take a position that perhaps requires some explanation. With due respect for forty years' worth of critical discourse on the contested concept of "meaning," as it relates to architecture, meaning is, simply, about the significance that a building or space comes to hold for an individual through its use. Engagement with a building or place is related at one level to the abstract matter of spatial sensation—of how one feels in a building or place. At another level, it is a matter of the tactile import of the many small, unremarkable physical interactions that make up the day: a transition in flooring that is subtly registered by the feet; the heft of a long industrial door as it slides along its track; the warmth of sunlight spilling into workspace; the pleasingly regular texture of corrugated metal; the smooth polished surface of a knob on the raw steel of a door. The experience of architecture is the sum of moments of this sort, and its meaning—its import, or the imprint it leaves on one's physical memory—derives from the *quality* of that experience.

Berke aims to make buildings that engender simultaneously unobtrusive and memorable architectural encounters. A completed building, she maintains, should first evince a "sense of 'rightness,' the sense that it could not have been made otherwise," that it is the uniquely appropriate response to the conditions of its time and place. This rightness, which imparts to the finished design a quality of inevitability,

Battery Park City Parks Conservancy, New York, New York, 1994–96. Glass pavers embedded in the concrete floor allow light to pass between the two levels.

Baron & Baron Inc., New York, New York, 1992–93, 1998. Sliding steel-and-glass doors in foreground and at far right

Rogers & Goffigon, Greenwich, Connecticut, 1998–99, 2002–3. Cutting and packing area

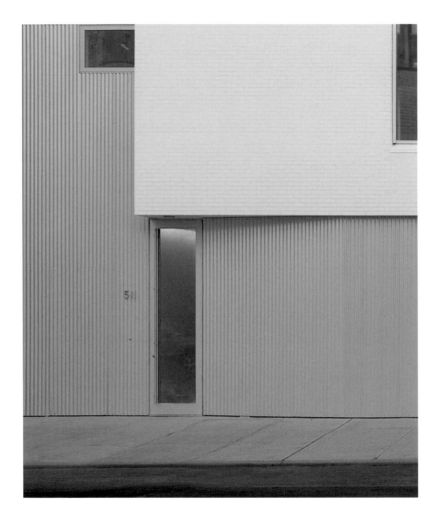

is necessary for the work to make a singular and indelible impression. In what she thinks of as a kind of revelatory moment, the architecture prompts a second look as the user comes to recognize the hand of an architect at work. As a result of this personal discovery, the architecture becomes memorable and, Berke hopes, artfully powerful.

In the final analysis—quite literally, when the clinical exercise of parsing the context, form, and materiality of Berke's buildings is done—what most endures in one's memory of her projects is the intensely satisfying settings they provide. Her work can induce a strong desire to linger in the space, to consume it, to allow its ambient qualities to seep in. While the experience of architecture and the feelings to which it can give rise are difficult to describe, a few sketches are suggestive.

———

Approaching the Hope Branch Library from across the town's green, I am struck by the thought that it epitomizes Berke's desire to leave a mark on the landscape that is distinct but not necessarily recognizable as the product of her hand. While the library's scale, brick construction, and metal awnings blend perfectly into the context of vernacular commercial structures on one side and the 1950s bank branch on the other, its sloped, zinc-clad light monitor imparts to the building an air of contemporaneity that sets it apart from its neighbors. I can imagine a passerby discerning something unique in this library, without quite being able to name it. The interior conveys the same sense of a subtly subverted familiarity: although it has the general aspect of a straightforward box occupied by ranks of bookcases and other typical furniture, its sloping ceiling of Douglas fir and the entrance and checkout station rendered in varying widths of maple boards and paneling inject an element of surprise that enhances the simple act of going to the library.

———

In an open, well-lit space at one end of the former factory that houses Elizabeth Eakins Inc, a company that designs and hand-makes cotton and wool rugs, a woman winds wool yarn into skeins on a swift as she chats with her co-workers. Across the floor, dyers boil pots of wool in a room with multiple glass doors that contain odors but permit the dyers to visually connect with their colleagues. Other women sit on an enormous low platform in the middle of the building, assembling and ironing cotton rugs. At lunch, employees come together in the kitchen, the physical heart of a company that they describe as being like

Hope Branch Library, Hope, Indiana, 1994–98

Elizabeth Eakins Inc, South Norwalk, Connecticut, 2000–2001. Rug-assembly platform

a second family. One woman says, "I've been here for six years, and there's not a day that I wake up and think, 'I'm not going to work.' I love it: I look forward to coming and doing what I do." Others comment on the cheering effect of the building's copious light and space.[1]

———

On a brilliant, brisk winter day, I visit the owners of a small but perfectly proportioned and articulated house on an island in Long Island Sound. Composed of two slightly offset volumes connected by an enclosed breezeway, and sheathed in white cedar siding that is weathering to a warm gray, the house immediately impresses with the stripped-down grace of its form. The interior features elements that satisfy a love of the purest form of modernism: an open living/dining space, walls and cabinetry painted white, contrasting touches of elegance in the form of black stone countertops and dark-stained oak floors, a wall of glass doors that admit a flood of light. The house strikes one as perfectly at home in the surrounding woods and exudes an engulfing sense of tranquility and repose.

———

The Yale School of Art occupies two buildings: a disused community center attributed to Louis Kahn and renovated by Berke, and a new building that Berke constructed on a snug adjacent site. Art school is a dichotomous affair, alternately solitary and social in nature: students retire to studios for the messy job of making art and periodically come together in galleries and critique spaces to show and discuss their work. This duality is approximated architecturally both externally and in the interior at Yale. The narrow alley approaches along the sides of the buildings exert a physical pressure that might be likened to the spatial containment of the studio; similarly, the knob of space between the two structures is a kind of relief valve, allowing for physical mixing in much the same way that the galleries and critique rooms offer social release from the solitude of the studio. Internally, the organization of spaces produces a pattern that disperses student workspaces and communal areas in both plan and section, rather than locating all studios on one floor, all galleries on another floor, and so on. Berke's selection of simple, neutral materials that can withstand whatever the students might inflict on them plainly foregrounds the spaces' users and the art they produce. At the same time, her retention of certain elements of the original community center—for example, a wall of the swimming pool, now the site of the graduate photography critique room—lends the building the air of a palimpsest, on which each generation of users will inscribe a new layer of meaning.

———

What do these sketches reveal about the manner in which an architectural encounter produces satisfaction or meaning, and about Berke's attitude toward the use of the spaces the firm creates? One of the characteristics the projects in this section share is that, in most cases, the materials employed are unremarkable: galvanized metal, concrete block, brick, and plywood, among others. Although this is occasionally a matter of economy, Berke's utilization of ordinary materials usually is a matter of choice. While she does not shy away from employing more lavish materials when budget and program permit or the client desires it, the firm generally favors materials that wear well, and these tend to be "things that are industrial in origin, humble in origin, anti-precious."[2]

This attitude toward materials immediately calls to mind Berke's notion of the everyday. The notion assumes a different kind of significance, however, in the context of the relationship between use and architectural meaning that is asserted here, and in regard to a typology that has increasingly captured the firm's interest: the workplace. The firm believes that a project is not complete until it is inhabited. Berke explains, "Places where things happen, times when our buildings get used and worked over and invigorated, are the fulfillment of those buildings for us, not the last coat of paint before the owner arrives."[3] This belief accounts in part for the intrigue that the everyday and the workplace have held for DBPA over the years. To Berke, the workplace is the last refuge of the everyday. "The regular stuff of life," as she describes it, is intimately tied to workspace, which she thinks of as "an architecture that survives, even revels in, its occupation." Labor and the clutter or disorder that often accompany it do not diminish workspace, but enhance it. The workplace, then, is a site in which space comes to be invested with architectural meaning through labor—that is, through use.

The firm believes that it is possible for architectural design to ennoble the workplace without appearing to condescend to or patronize the worker, citing as a model the factory buildings that Albert Kahn designed for the automobile industry in the early twentieth century. Consideration of the nature of labor has led Berke to a conception of the workplace that repositions it within the social hierarchy:

It's difficult to talk about this, because the language is loaded. I think that work gives meaning and structure to your life. And I

Yale School of Art, Yale University, New Haven, Connecticut, 1997–2000. Juncture of new building (left) and the renovated building (right)

feel that in our culture, we have demeaned most work to be drudgery. I don't think it has to be that way. Work isn't always fun, but I think that work can almost always be fulfilling. And if it isn't from the actual thing that you do, it can be from the relationships with your co-workers and the existence of another community that is neither your family nor the place where you live nor the place where you worship, if that's part of your life. I would like to contribute to that; I'd like to try out these ideas. But all the ideas come out of a genuine belief in the power and value of work.[4]

It would be easy to dismiss Berke's conviction as an earnest expression of the modernist trope of architecture as social salvation. At the least, it calls for a definition of the term "ennobling workspace," which denotes architecture that endows its users with a sense of dignity, provides sensory and psychic satisfaction, and facilitates personal connectivity. Elizabeth Eakins Inc illustrates this with nearly indexical precision: employees find great pleasure in the space, feel strongly bonded to each other, and emanate a quiet confidence. Berke's design of the headquarters for the Battery Park City Parks Conservancy, which maintains and programs the outdoor amenities at Battery Park City in lower Manhattan, engenders similar qualities and experiences in its users. One employee speaks of a "fusion" of the conservancy's work and the space Berke designed for it and believes that the physical environment "puts people at ease and helps foster cohesive collaboration between departments."[5]

The foregoing descriptions of workspaces that appear to have ennobling qualities raise basic questions about the nature of such spaces. Is it the culture of an organization or the space's architectural character that ennobles the workplace? Is workspace in some way fundamentally different from other kinds of spaces or buildings? The answers lead back to the sources of meaning and coherence in Berke's architecture.

Designing ennobling workspace requires a client who values the qualities associated with this term—one who feels it important that

employees derive satisfaction from their space and believes that the culture of work subsumes and transcends mere labor. The dignity of a workspace is thus the result of a confluence of design ideals with a specific idea of what makes for a rewarding environment. This is no more true of workspace, however, than it is of any other type of space. The creation of places that exalt workers and work requires not the reinvention of architectural language or principles, but a rethinking of architectural entitlement and the matter of how workspace assumes meaning for its occupants. For Berke, architectural meaning derives in the workplace, as it does in all typologies, from the quotidian: the ordinary acts and small moments that perhaps go unnoticed but nonetheless leave their trace in the form of an experiential memory. The sensibility and intentions that ground Berke's ideas about workspace lie at the heart of *all* her work and yield a common, consistent result: the creation of architecture that, through active, invigorating engagement, stirs in its user a sense that it is just as it ought to be.

NOTES
1. Staff of Elizabeth Eakins Inc, interviews by the author, Jan. 27, 2006.
2. Deborah Berke, Maitland Jones, and Marc Leff, interview by the author, Oct. 16, 2006.
3. Ibid.
4. Ibid.
5. Neil Utterback, executive assistant, Battery Park City Parks Conservancy, interview by the author, March 7, 2005.

Battery Park City Parks Conservancy. Workshop

Irwin Union Bank, Columbus, Indiana, 2004–6. Drive-through side of the bank

Box Studios

New York, New York
2002–4

The headquarters of Box Studios, a photography studio specializing in digital retouching and production for fashion photographers, magazines, and artists, is a nineteenth-century industrial building in New York's Meatpacking District. The structure's three floors total 17,500 square feet of workspaces, meeting rooms, and administrative spaces. In Berke's crisp interpretation of industrial architecture, the exposed-timber-and-brick construction has been transformed into a high-tech, modern facility that meets the client's stringent technical requirements. On the exterior, the new muted façade, with its grid of steel-sash windows and black-painted brick, reinvents this old structure for the digital work that takes place inside.

Berke organized Box Studios along two axes. A new skylight and light well puncture all three floors, defining a vertical axis and bringing light through the center of the space down to the ground floor. On each level, programmatic elements are disposed on either side of a central longitudinal axis—literally inscribed in the concrete on the first floor, and more conceptually grounded on the second and third floors. Distribution of the program is determined by the lighting requirements at each stage of production. Complementing the axial organization is a sectional segmentation: public areas are confined to the front of the building, while production facilities occupy the rest of it, resulting in a figurative cleavage within the structure. Collectively, DBPA's strategies result in a seemingly simple building that accommodates multiple hierarchies.

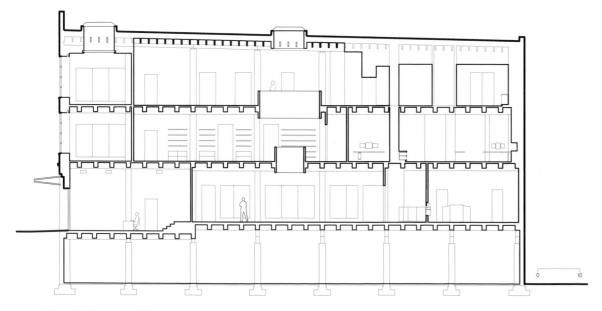

A skylight and telescoping light well illuminate the entire section.

Berke refined an implied nine-square grid in the original façade to create a new elevation that projects an image of order.

The concrete floor of the first level is saw-cut down the middle, from the lobby (shown here) through the entire length of the building.

The light well terminates in the ceiling of the first floor and is centered on the editing and packing studio. Reminders of previous commercial occupants of the building—butchers and printers, among others—survive in the exposed timber construction.

Production and administrative spaces are dispersed around the light well on the second floor. The daylit viewing room is beyond.

View through the light well, from the third floor to the print table on the first floor. Floors on the second and third levels are of painted wood, in contrast to the concrete finish on the first floor.

The digital retouching studio is isolated from natural light.

Light floods the third-floor viewing room through three skylights as well as the expansive new windows.

Owner's office

Scanning room

Modica Market

Seaside, Florida
1988, 1991

Berke was among the earliest architects to construct buildings at Seaside, the first community developed according to the principles of what is now known as New Urbanism. Individually and with Carey McWhorter, she produced eighteen projects there. While the master plan and design code, modeled after traditional prewar American towns, might have led Berke into the lair of nostalgia, her projects instead reflect an attitude of restraint and lucidity. The architecture critic Martin Filler described Berke's houses as "bracing bits of lemon among the treacle" of Seaside.[1]

In addition to sixteen houses, Berke completed two commercial projects at Seaside. Per-spi-cas-ity, an outdoor market composed of nine small stalls built of plywood with canvas awnings, is located close to the beach. Berke's second commercial project, Modica Market, sits across Seaside's main thoroughfare from Per-spi-cas-ity and on the town square, which also features buildings by Steven Holl and Machado & Silvetti, among other prominent architects. Modica encompasses an unusual mixed-use program of grocery store/café and community meeting room. The 5,000-square-foot structure occupies a wedge-shaped site with limited frontage on the square. The L-shaped plan of the store maximizes its exposure to the street, and large steel-and-glass windows on the façade expand its sense of openness. The store hugs the community room,

Awnings at the front of the market are cantilevered between columns and do not touch the façade.

The simple service entrance to the market (right) contrasts with the symmetrical, slightly more formal entrance to the community meeting room (left). Awnings at all entrances are fabricated of the same corrugated metal as the building's skin. Both elevations are punched with deep, aluminum-sash windows. A mixed-use facility designed by Steven Holl (far left) adjoins Modica Market.

which is reached from a separate entrance at the rear of the building.

Modica Market was Berke's most cogent articulation to date of her notion of an architecture of the everyday. In both materials and the organization of retail activity, Modica Market is about the enjoyment of ordinary things and experiences. The building sits on a base of concrete block and is clad in corrugated galvanized aluminum; skylights in the community room are fitted out with standard win-

dows. Inside, tactile and visual textures are produced in part by the exposed roof structure and decking but primarily by the products themselves, which are packed chockablock on the floor-to-ceiling shelves. The contrast of this density with the double-height store's spaciousness creates an environment that is at once bustling, relaxed, and agreeably unremarkable.

NOTE
1. Martin Filler, "Model Houses," *House & Garden* (April 1989), 44.

Texture in the market is provided by products, which fill every available inch of shelf space. Industrial garage-style doors at the front of the building roll up on their tracks to open the store to the square.

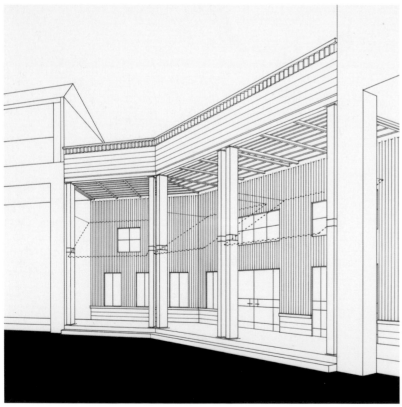

Top: Community meeting room. Walls of plywood maintain the building's minimal, economical materials palette. Above the datum established by the plywood, perforated corrugated metal lined with batting provides acoustical insulation.

Above: Initial façade concept

Opposite: Entrance façade of community meeting space

Hope Branch Library

Hope, Indiana
1994–98

Located on the square of a classic small town about fifteen miles north of Columbus, Indiana, this branch of the Bartholomew County Public Library serves a community of 2,500 people. The building's context is simultaneously predictable and surprising. The square, which is a public park, is flanked on all sides by the typical variety of churches, stores, and services found in a village. The presence of Berke's branch library and, next to it, a branch of Irwin Union Bank designed by Harry Weese (1958) is an unexpected infusion of modern architecture into this traditional townscape. The Hope Branch Library is a product of the Cummins Engine Foundation's architecture program, which was established in 1957 and pays architects' fees so that public buildings in Bartholomew County may be designed by prominent members of the field.

DBPA's 6,000-square-foot building takes important cues from its context. Its brick walls and modest height relate to Weese's bank, while its steel windows and metal awnings connect it to other neighboring commercial structures. The tall windows on the north and west façades dissolve the boundary between the public space of the street and the library's interior and, together with the long sweeping zinc-clad clerestory, admit generous amounts of light.

Although extremely simple in plan and architectural language, the library plays an important civic role beyond its strict programmatic function. It serves as an after-school gathering center in this small town and is designed to be particularly child-friendly. In addition, at all times of day it is frequented by elderly residents. In a place that describes itself as "a surprising little town," Berke's library is, in a sense, the architectural glue that binds the community.

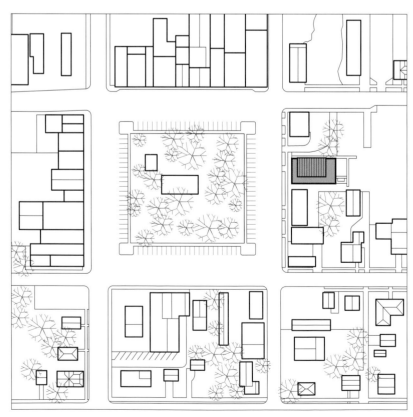

The building's north façade is extensively fenestrated to provide light for all-day reading without relying on artificial illumination. The awnings on the clerestory shield the interior from the western sun and, like the clerestory, are made of zinc that has developed a blue-gray patina.

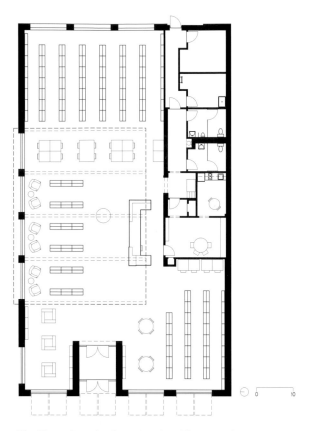

The library is a simple rectangle, with spaces for checkout and administrative offices, tables and seating, and stacks to hold its 20,000 volumes.

View from entrance toward the stacks. The roof is expressed on the building's interior as a sloping ceiling of Douglas fir supported by laminated timber beams.

Wood boards and paneling of differing widths establish a hierarchy of vertical rhythms at the checkout area. Nearly all the materials were sourced from local manufacturers.

Berke's library and Weese's bank, viewed from the park. The library's clerestory contrasts with the pyramidal wood domes of the bank's roof.

Battery Park City Parks Conservancy

New York, New York
1994–96

Built on ninety-two acres of landfill that replaced deteriorated shipping piers on the western side of lower Manhattan, Battery Park City is a development of commercial, residential, recreational, and cultural uses begun in 1980. The master plan required that 30 percent of the site be reserved as open space, and since 1985 thirteen parks, gardens, playgrounds, and plazas have been created for public enjoyment. Planting, programming, and maintenance of these amenities are the responsibility of the Battery Park City Parks Conservancy, whose first headquarters Berke formed out of space on the ground floor and basement of an apartment tower.

The project's site and program were intriguingly divergent: the space was originally intended by the building's owners to contain a movie theater, while the brief specified offices, conference rooms, workshops, and storage for horticulturalists, maintenance workers, recreation programmers, and administrators. DBPA's two

challenges were to bring natural light into as much of the space as possible and to organize the program in a way that simultaneously accommodates the diverse staff needs and sustains a sense of community. One of the firm's solutions fulfilled both objectives: double-height voids at the two perimeter walls allow light to reach the lower level and act as sectional connectors, creating visual links between the offices on the ground floor and the workshops and equipment storage areas below. Deeper within the space, glass pavers embedded in the floor of the office level filter light into the workshops.

If the vertical voids bring a certain spatial poetry to BPC Parks' quarters, then the no-nonsense materials, furnishings, and fixtures, including concrete block, sturdy maple furniture, and industrial lighting, are reminders that this is a workspace, designed for messiness and durability. Ultimately, it is precisely the work—the hum of the staff's activity—that defines this place.

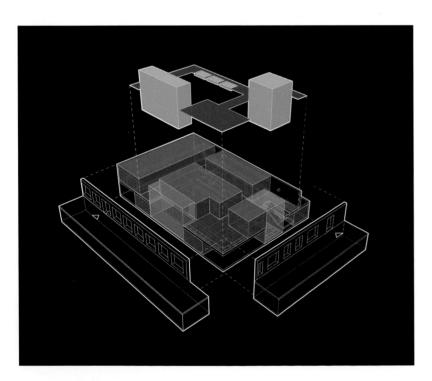

Double-height voids on the perimeter walls allow light to reach workspaces on the lower level. The voids also provide visual connections across these spaces and between the two floors.

The conference room and lunchroom feature maple built-ins, designed by Berke, which are meant to both withstand and reveal their wear. Windows frame the view from the conference room across the basement workspace, toward the conservancy's entrance.

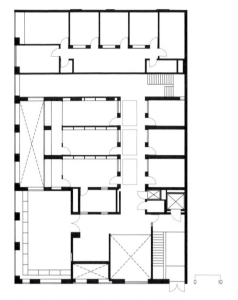

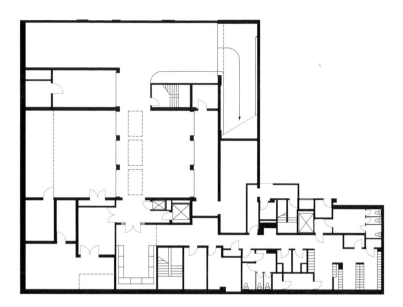

Openings in the first floor (marked by an X in the plan above) admit light into the lower level.

Lower-level plan

Staff offices flank both sides of the corridor, which features industrial light fixtures and built-in maple furniture. The corridor terminates at the southern double-height void, the lower level of which is occupied by a lounge for the groundskeepers.

View from the entrance across the daylit lower-level workspace, toward the conference room/lunchroom

Groundskeepers' workspace

Elizabeth Eakins Inc

South Norwalk, Connecticut
2000–2001

Elizabeth Eakins, a designer and maker of several lines of hand-woven, all-natural and organic wool and cotton rugs, commissioned Berke to convert a 22,000-square-foot former floor-wax factory into offices, a design studio, yarn-dyeing and hand-weaving rooms, a carpet-assembly area, and warehouse storage. The company functions like a family, and Eakins required a configuration that would provide appropriate spaces for the firm's separate divisions (cotton and wool) but also satisfy the staff's desire to commingle and work together. Berke completely gutted the building and

stripped it down to its steel-and-concrete-block structure, allowing her to organize the program in a plan that simultaneously fulfills Eakins's dual needs and corresponds to the production process.

To create discrete areas within the hollowed-out volume, Berke inserted three programmatically distinct twelve-foot-high boxes arranged symmetrically around the entrance. The central box, which contains the kitchen and lavatories, is flanked by boxes housing offices that support the company's two branches; the offices, in turn, are the gateway to their respective divisions' production areas. The production cycle reaches its conclusion on the 3,300-square-foot

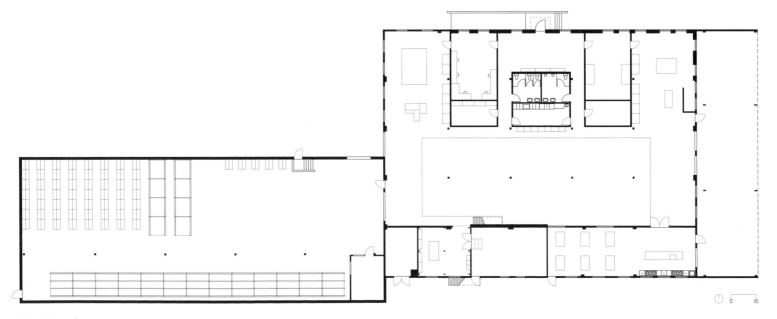

First-floor plan

Berke installed a composition of new aluminum-sash windows. The double row at left marks the workspace of the wool division.

rug-assembly platform, which sits like a shallow island in the middle of the building. Beyond, the dyeing kitchen and weaving studio that supply the raw material for the wool division share an appropriately well-lit space.

To meet the project's very modest budget, DBPA retained existing building elements and employed reclaimed materials wherever possible. Rolling fire doors were preserved, for example, and the assembly platform was constructed of oak strips salvaged from a bowling alley. More than just tactics for economizing, however, these acts of environmental responsibility exemplify a particular business culture: the company thinks of its enterprise as a life-style that values sustainability, insists on respectful treatment of employees, and encourages professional growth and adeptness at multiple jobs. The quiet productivity and spirit of collegiality that suffuse the atmosphere at Elizabeth Eakins Inc find their architectural corollary in the openness, frankness, and warmth of the building's space.

Entrance lobby. The low height of the gypsum boxes Berke inserted to define distinct spaces preserves a sense of openness. Berke retained the original sprinkler valve for its sculptural qualities.

Dyeing kitchen. Wool yarn is dyed in large pots of boiling pigmented water—a process that demands great accuracy to achieve consistency in color. Tall, wide windows provide natural light, making it easier for the dyers to monitor color.

In the wool division, employees handcraft custom textiles from wool that has been dyed and woven on-site.

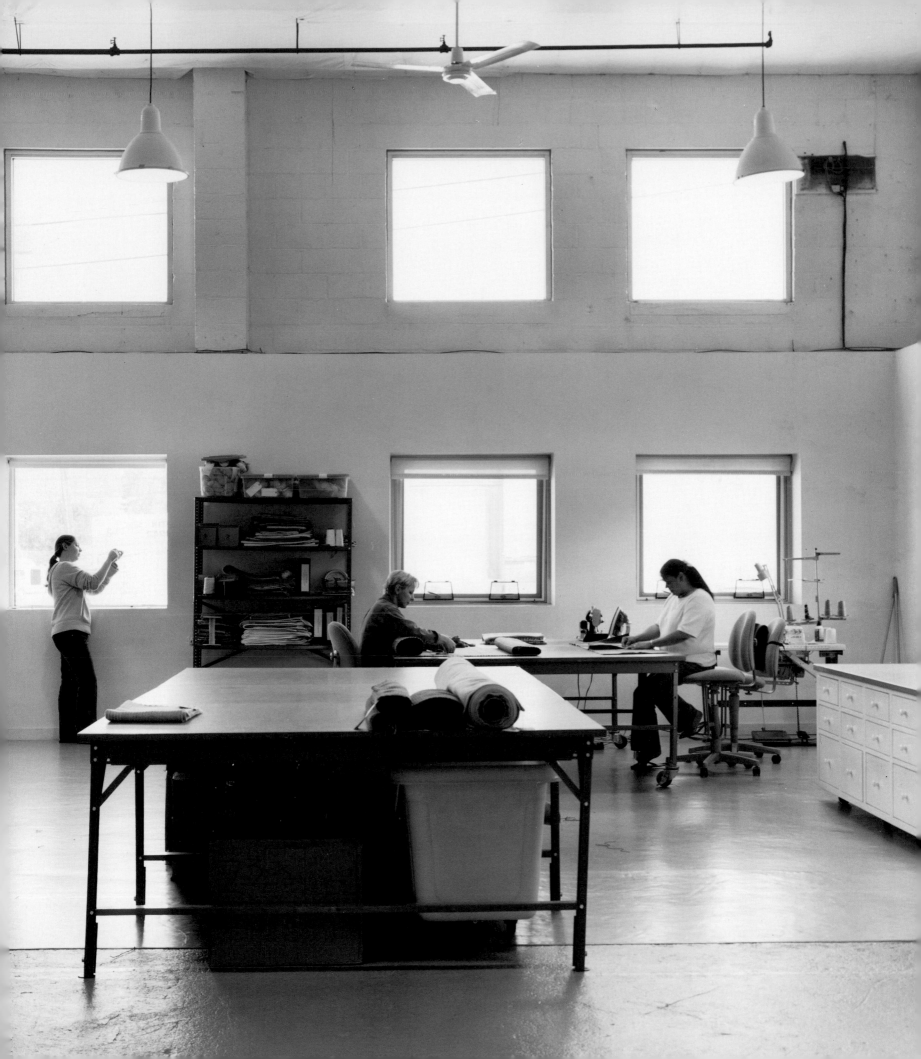

Above: Second-floor office

Opposite: Dyeing kitchen and weaving studio. Once dyed, the wool yarn is handwoven on floor looms. The ventilating system—which, on temperate days, can be complemented by opening the rolling door—rids the space of fumes produced by the dyeing process and fiber dust generated by weaving. In addition to retaining the rolling fire door, Berke salvaged the industrial light shades.

The production space opens into the warehouse. Recycling wood from a bowling alley to construct the rug-assembly platform (foreground), repairing the existing concrete floor, and reconditioning lighting fixtures found in the building allowed Berke to effect both financial and environmental benefits.

Shelter Island House No. 1

Shelter Island, New York
2001–3

This 1,200-square-foot residence, in a quiet town on an island in Long Island Sound, was commissioned by a couple who sought a simplified lifestyle that nonetheless left room for personal expression. Berke responded with a two-bedroom, two-bath home that is infused with the aesthetic of an urban loft. The two rectilinear offset volumes that comprise it— one containing living, dining, and guest/study spaces, the other the master suite—are connected by a small glassed-in room that opens to become a breezeway in the summer. Sheathed in white cedar siding, the house presents a taciturn face to the street, its minimal fenestration offering no hint of the light-filled interiors it harbors. Two-thirds of the larger volume is given over to an open space, where a tall cabinet unit loosely separates the kitchen from the living and dining areas. The rear façade of this long room is dominated by sliding glass doors that reveal the site's best view: a wooded area with a hollow to the immediate south of the house.

In addition to the white cedar siding, galvanized metal roofing and brushed aluminum windows were chosen for their ability to wear to pleasing tones of gray that will imbue the house with the sense that it is in harmony with its natural setting. Inside, the chasteness of white surfaces is relieved by black stone countertops, dark-stained oak floors, and a teak dining table designed by DBPA. The effect is of a perfectly balanced haven of tranquility.

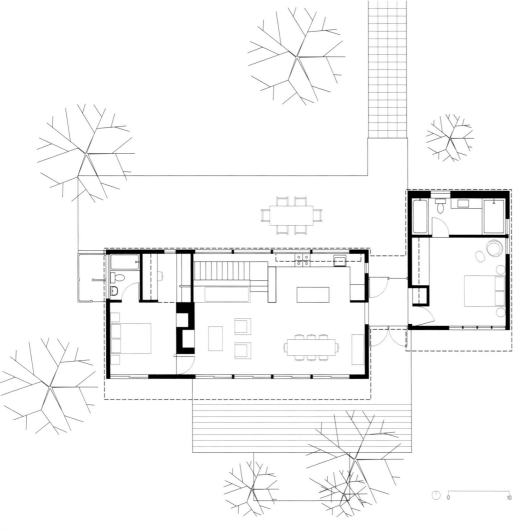

Street façade. Subtle, limited fenestration preserves the mural integrity of this side of the building. The front "lawn," intentionally left without vegetation, is a kind of landscape analogue to the house's restrained front elevation.

Clerestory windows admit light and fresh air to the kitchen and living/dining area. Black stone countertops add a note of contrast to the pristine kitchen environment.

The living/dining space is visually continuous with the guest suite beyond. A thick wall separating the two spaces encloses a fireplace on the public side and built-in cabinets and shelves on the guest-room side.

In the master bedroom, casement windows open onto the woods behind the house.

Yale School of Art

Yale University
New Haven, Connecticut
1997–2000

Berke's building at Yale University, Holcombe T. Green Jr. Hall, which serves as the home for the School of Art and includes the School of Drama's New Theater, was the first completed under the university's Arts Area Master Plan of 1994. Green Hall provides facilities purpose-built for undergraduate art programs and graduate painting, photography, and graphic design programs. The project brief called for the renovation of an existing building and construction of a new freestanding facility on an adjacent lot to accommodate these disciplines as well as the drama school's New Theater and its supporting functions.

DBPA faced several design challenges. The deteriorated existing building, New Haven's former Jewish Community Center, which is attributed to Louis Kahn, was in some ways fundamentally incompatible with the new uses to which it would be put. Berke imaginatively converted athletic facilities to new roles—the gymnasium, for instance, became the graphic design department, and the pool was transformed into space for photography critiques—while retaining as many of the old structure's original features as possible. To create a single school from two volumes that are linked in use and spirit but physically separate, the firm employed a strategy that

exploited both plan and section. In plan, the front of Berke's new structure laps the rear of the Kahn building, creating an interstitial space that is the architectural equivalent of the center of a Venn diagram. Each of the school's programs occupies its own double-height space, resulting in sectional complexity that carries from the existing building to its new counterpart and establishes an abstract connection between them.

The project brief also laid out the particular requirements of facilities for making art: natural light, clean surfaces that neither dictate medium nor limit dimension, and spaces of various scales, contained within an architecturally neutral environment that affords both the solitude that cultivates creativity and opportunities for the communal interaction that reinforces individual inventiveness. To provide maximum illumination, Berke's structure incorporates tall vertical windows and long ribbons of windows, and the existing building's perimeter walls were opened so that every studio has natural light. Concrete floors and plaster walls are the principal elements of the unobtrusive interior materials palette. Ample room for display and review are the magnets that draw students from their individual zones. Whether large or intimate, shared or private, the spaces of the School of Art and New Theater are background for the work done within them.

The Yale School of Art and New Theater occupy an irregularly shaped swath of a block between Chapel and Crown Streets. Berke's new building (left) faces Crown Street; the former Jewish Community Center, attributed to Louis Kahn, fronts on Chapel Street. In order to maximize the footprint of the new building within the trapezoidal block, Berke pared away its northeast corner, creating a small courtyard where the new and old structures nearly meet.

216

Crown Street façade. The building is composed of a restrained materials palette of light gray brick and glass curtain walls articulated by aluminum mullions. Slight variegations in the brick produce a random pattern that contrasts with the consistent, repeated rhythm of the fenestration.

In its somewhat gritty context of unassuming structures, the new art school induces a double take: although it clearly evidences the hand of a designer, its lack of pretensions make it a natural fit for its milieu.

Students present their work for review and exhibition in this gallery/critique space in the new structure. Although it is situated primarily below grade, its openness to the first floor above encourages casual observation and social exchange.

Windows vary among the thirty-five studios in the Crown Street building, and the differing lighting conditions provide the means by which students distinguish and choose their spaces. Some windows extend in a band from wall to wall; others span from floor to ceiling; and a few studios are windowless. Neutral, sturdy materials provide an appropriate—and durable—setting for art making.

The new building's east wall faces an industrial red-brick structure. A path between the two buildings leads from Crown Street to the courtyard between them, producing a sequence of compression yielding to expansion.

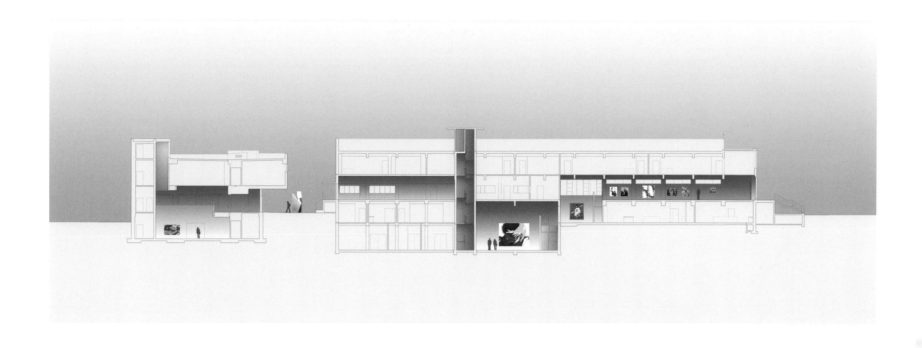

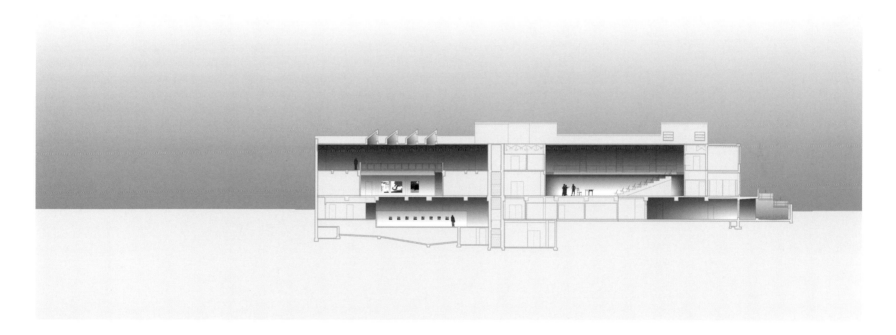

Top: North-south section through the western half of the former Jewish Community Center and the new building. The original building is entered from Chapel Street (far right), a half-floor above street level. Gallery spaces here unfold in section in a series of cascading, interlocking spaces. The long first-floor exhibition space gives way via a stair to a ground-floor gallery. Another staircase in turn gives access to the principal, double-height gallery, created by combining former handball courts in the basement. Offices occupy the first floor beyond the internal stair tower. Berke echoed the L-shaped section at the core of the old building in the new structure.

Above: North-south section through the eastern half of the old structure. DBPA renovated the two-story auditorium of the former community center into an experimental theater for the drama school. The 5,000-square-foot space also includes a public lobby with ticketing service on the first floor and, on the ground floor, a green room, dressing rooms, and backstage support facilities. The photography critique space, a half-floor below grade in the former pool, and the graphic design space, with its mezzanine, are in the rear half of the building.

Exterior view from the north. The walkway along the eastern edge of Kahn's building leads to the entrance to Berke's building. The fenestration on this elevation of the new structure varies ever so subtly from that of the south façade: while the two curtain walls are articulated in the same tripartite modules, the arrangements of the types of glass are inverted (see page 218).

Renovation of the exterior of the former Jewish Community Center included the replacement of the windows, marble spandrels, and stainless-steel mullions; the addition of an accessibility ramp; and the redesign of the stair rails. The new building alludes to the old in the composition of its elevations: in both, parapet walls of brick bracket a curtain-wall façade. Because Berke modified the proportions and materials of the windows and the thickness of brick walls in the new building, however, it is clearly distinguished from the existing structure.

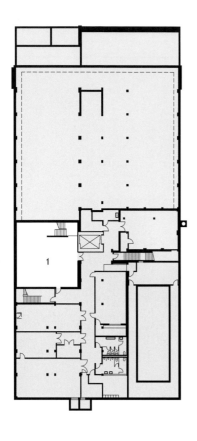

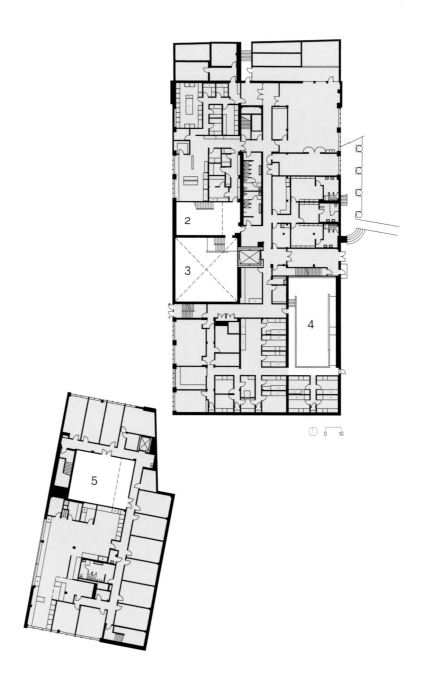

Basement plan. 1: Basement gallery

Ground-floor plan. 2: Ground-floor gallery. 3: Open to gallery below.
4: Photography critique space. 5: Painting critique space

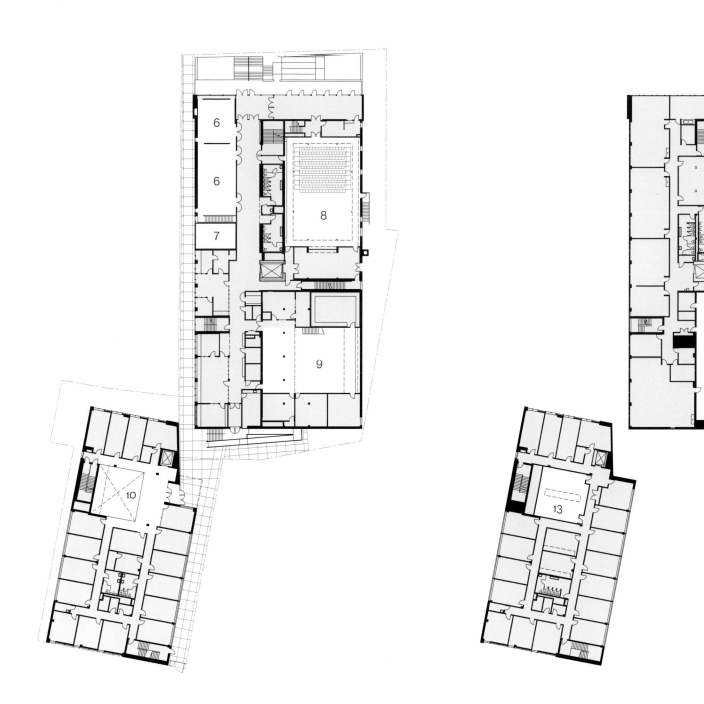

First-floor plan. 6: First-floor galleries. 7: Open to galleries below.
8: New Theater. 9: Graphic design common space. 10: Painting
critique space

Second-floor plan. 11: New Theater. 12: Graphic design mezzanine.
13: Painting common space

To convert the swimming pool into a studio for photography critiques, DBPA inserted a "liner" of plaster walls, leaving the green wall tiles, where possible, as evidence of the space's original use.

Double-height gallery for student work in the Kahn building. The steel lighting frame can be lowered to adjust illumination.

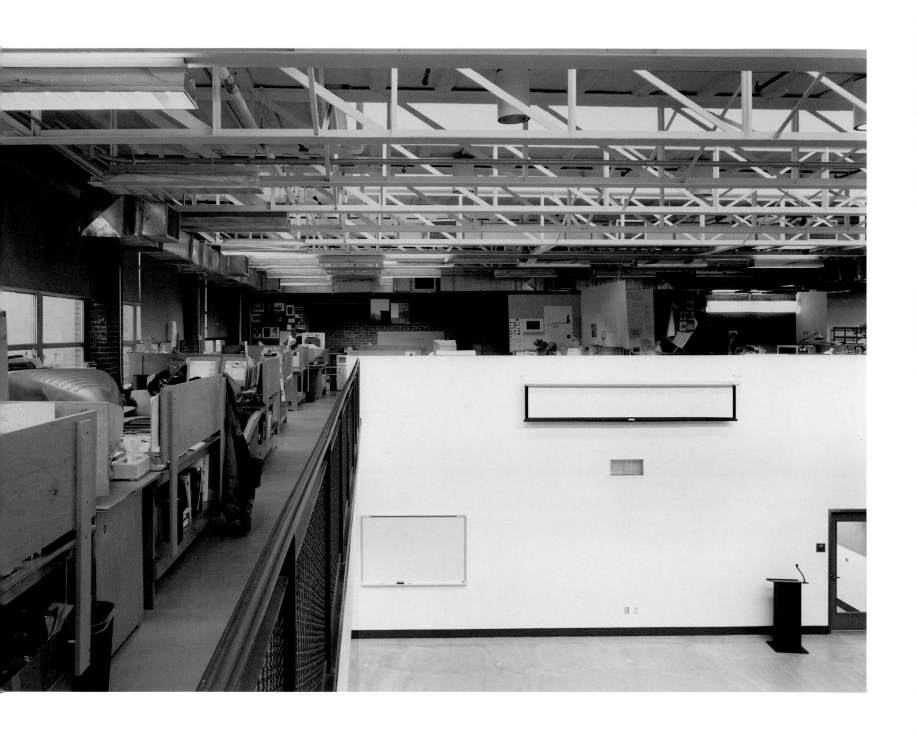

DBPA converted the old building's gymnasium into the graduate graphic design department, which is composed of a large presentation space on the first level (opposite) and a new mezzanine level for open studio space (above). Berke added light scoops in the roof (visible in the section drawing on page 223) to admit natural light to the studios, and the existing metal roof trusses were painted white to further enhance illumination.

The double-height black-box New Theater is clean and spare, its industrial quality the appropriate setting for experimentation.

Chapel Street façade of the former Jewish Community Center. Berke has expressed her admiration for Kahn's use of repetition and of reductive yet sophisticated materials, his mastery at "putting things together," and his "simple spaces that are somehow profound." Berke and her partners share with Kahn an ability to elicit the second look that slowly reveals the careful thought behind work that, on first glance, is deceptively simple.

Project List

DEP Shaft Maintenance Building
Renovation of New York City DEP facility
Brooklyn, New York
2008–present
Client: New York City Department of Design and
Construction. Structural Engineer: Robert Silman
Associates. MEP Engineer: Ambrosino, DePinto &
Schmieder. Sustainable Design Consultant: Viridian
Energy & Environmental. Historic Preservation
Consultant: Falk Associates. Lighting Designer: PHT
Lighting Design. Cost Estimator: Federman Design +
Construction Consulting

Narciso Rodriguez
Fashion design studio, showroom, and offices
New York, New York
2008 (unbuilt)
Client: Liz Claiborne Inc.

Dale Chihuly Gallery
Art gallery
Las Vegas, Nevada
2007–present
Client: MGM Mirage Design Group; Dale Chihuly
Studio. Structural Engineer: Halcrow Yolles.
MEP Engineer: Flack + Kurtz. Lighting Designer:
Renfro Design Group

535 Madison Avenue Plaza
Renovation of plaza and lobby
New York, New York
2007–present
Client: Park Tower Group. Landscape Architect: Zion
Breen & Richardson Associates. Lighting Designer:
Renfro Design Group

Lafayette Avenue House
Single-family residence
Greensboro, North Carolina
2007–present

North Moore Street Loft
Renovation
New York, New York
2007–present
General Contractor: TOG Construction

Reedy Creek Fire Station 2-B
Emergency services building
Lake Buena Vista, Florida
2007–present
Client: Reedy Creek Improvement District

Shartenberg Development
Interior design of 460-unit apartment building
New Haven, Connecticut
2007–present
Client: Becker + Becker. Executive Architect:
SLCE Architects

21c Museum Hotel
240-room hotel, restaurant, and
contemporary art museum
Austin, Texas
2007–present
Client: ACE Unlimited: Steve Wilson and Laura Lee
Brown; The Poe Companies. Executive Architect:
Goody Clancy. Architect of Record: Susman Tisdale
Gayle. Landscape Architect: Ten Eyck Landscape
Architects. Structural Engineer: Magnusson
Klemencic Associates. MEP Engineer: Newcomb &
Boyd. Specifications: Falk Associates

Moores Mill Road House
Single-family residence
Hopewell, New Jersey
2007
Builder: Princeton Design Guild

Seascape Lane House
Single-family residence
Sagaponack, New York
2007 (unbuilt)
Sustainable Design Consultant: Steven
Winter Associates

Sigerson Morrison Madison Avenue
Retail shoe and accessories boutique
New York, New York
2007
Client: Fisher Footwear. General Contractor: Rebcor.
Lighting Designer: Illumination Works

West Main Street Penthouse
Addition and interior design
Louisville, Kentucky
2007
Landscape Designer: Jon Carloftis. General
Contractor: Peters Construction

Epron Road House
Single-family residence
Salt Spring, British Columbia
2006–present

Forestwood Drive House
Single-family residence and artist's studio
Bahama, North Carolina
2006–present
General Contractor: A. G. Builders

Sarah's Way House No. 2
Single-family residence renovation and addition
Amagansett, New York
2006–present

Tulip Avenue House
Single-family residence
Llewellyn Park, New Jersey
2006–present
Landscape Architect: Zion Breen & Richardson
Associates. Structural Engineer: Ross Dalland PE.
Civil Engineer: Lehr Associates. General Contractor:
Drill Construction

West 76th Street Townhouse
Renovation, addition, and interior design
New York, New York
2006–present

Crosby Street Loft No. 2
Renovation
New York, New York
2006–8

48 Bond Street
18-unit condominium apartment building
New York, New York
2006–8
Owner's Representative: KMM Consultants. Architect
of Record: GF55 Partners. Structural Engineer:
Severud Associates. MEP Engineer: Simon Rodkin
Consulting Engineers. Façade Consultant: Consulting
Associates of New York. Acoustical Engineer:
Acoustic Dimensions. Construction Manager: DCR
Construction. Lighting Designer: Vortex Lighting

Crosby Street Penthouse
Renovation
New York, New York
2006–7
Landscape Architect: Gunn Landscapes. Structural
and MEP Engineer: Becht Engineering. General
Contractor: ZZZ Carpentry. Interior Design: Kenneth
Alpert Design Group. Lighting Designer: Renfro Design
Group. Code Consultant: J. Callahan Consulting

Florida Case Study House
House design for *HOME* magazine's case study
house program, The New Florida Home
2006
Client: *HOME* magazine

Gymnasium
Boarding-school athletic building
Springfield, Massachusetts
2006 (unbuilt)
Client: The MacDuffie School

Walnut Street High-Rise
Conceptual design for a mixed-use complex
for an urban university
Philadelphia, Pennsylvania
2006

Hudson Street Loft
Renovation and interior design
New York, New York
2005–7
Structural Engineer: Ross Dalland PE. MEP Engineer:
Becht Engineering. General Contractor: Sweeney +
Conroy. Lighting Designer: Renfro Design Group

Arverne East Master Plan
Urban design for Arverne neighborhood in
Rockaway, Queens, including 1,500 residential
units and a retail core
Rockaway, New York
2005–6
Client: City Investment Fund. Collaborating
Architect: Handel Architects. Landscape Architect:
Sasaki Associates

The James
Renovation and expansion of 297-room hotel,
restaurant, spa, and nightclub
Chicago, Illinois
2005–6
Client: James Hotels. Architect of Record: Cubellis
MGDF. Structural Engineer: Thornton-Tomasetti
Group. MEP Engineer: Cosentini Associates. General
Contractor: Crane Construction Company. Lighting
Designer: Isometrix

Jay Street Building and Atelier
Renovation and interior design
New York, New York
2005–6
Landscape Architect: Gunn Landscapes. Structural
Engineer: Ross Dalland PE. MEP Engineer: Becht
Engineering. General Contractor: ZZZ Carpentry.
Lighting Designer: Renfro Design Group.

Burton Snowboards SoHo
Retail store
New York, New York
2005
Client: Burton Snowboards. MEP Engineer: Becht
Engineering. Construction Manager: Turner Interiors.
Lighting Designer: Renfro Design Group

River House
Residential compound
Bedford, New York
2004–present
Structural and MEP Engineer: Buro Happold
Consulting Engineers. General Contractor: Brenner
Builders. Lighting Designer: Renfro Design Group

Chappaquonsett Cottages
Single-family residence guest cottages
Tisbury, Massachusetts
2004–8
Structural Engineer: Sourati Engineering Group. Civil
Engineer: Schofield Barbini & Hoehn. Environmental
Engineer: Woods Hole Group. General Contractor:
DeSorcy Company

Joray Road House
Single-family residence and interior design
Ellsworth, Connecticut
2004–7
Structural Engineer: Ross Dalland PE. MEP Engineer:
Becht Engineering. General Contractor: Rick McCue.
Lighting Designer: Renfro Design Group

Marianne Boesky Gallery
Art gallery building
New York, New York
2004–7
Client: Marianne Boesky Gallery. Structural and
MEP Engineer: Buro Happold Consulting Engineers.
Civil Engineer: Philip Habib & Associates. General
Contractor: Eurostruct Inc. Lighting Designer: Renfro
Design Group. Cost Estimator: Federman Design +
Construction Consulting

Arrowhead Way House
Single-family residence
Darien, Connecticut
2004–6
Structural Engineer: Ross Dalland PE. General
Contractor: J & J Custom Builders. Interior
Design: Shaun Jackson. Lighting Designer: Renfro
Design Group

Georgica Road House
Single-family residence
East Hampton, New York
2004–6
Landscape Architect: Perry Guillot. Structural
Engineer: Ross Dalland PE. General Contractor:
Guzewicz Builders. Interior Design: FORM Architects

Irwin Union Bank, Creekview Branch
Branch bank
Columbus, Indiana
2004–6
Client: Irwin Union Bank. Architect of Record:
Todd Williams & Associates. Structural Engineer:
McComas Engineering. MEP Engineer: R. E. Dimond
& Associates. Civil Engineer: Columbus Surveying
& Engineering. General Contractor: Force
Construction Company

Shelter Island House No. 2
Single-family residence
Shelter Island, New York
2004–5
Structural Engineer: Lawrence Tuthill. General
Contractor: Mill Creek Builders

**Food & Shelter: Urban Farming and
Affordable Homes**
New Housing New York Design Ideas
Competition
Queens, New York
2004

GAV
Clothing design studio and showroom
New York, New York
2004
Client: Grossman & Vreeland. Structural, MEP, and
Acoustical Engineer: Lilker Associates. General
Contractor: Sweet Construction. Code Consultant:
JAM Consulting

Gardiner's Bay House No. 2
Single-family residence
Amagansett, New York
2003–8 (unbuilt)
Structural Engineer: Ross Dalland PE. MEP Engineer:
Becht Engineering. Civil Engineer: S. L. Maresca
Consulting Engineers. Environmental Consultant:
Inter-Science Research Associates

Liberty Street Loft
Renovation and interior design
New York, New York
2003–5
Mechanical Engineer: Becht Engineering. General
Contractor: ZZZ Carpentry. Code Consultant:
J. Callahan Consulting

James Hotel Scottsdale
Renovation and expansion of 200-room hotel,
restaurant, spa, and bar
Scottsdale, Arizona
2003–4
Client: James Hotels. Architect of Record:
DLR Group. Landscape Architect: Ten Eyck Landscape
Architects. Structural Engineer: Paul Koehler
Consulting Engineers. MEP Engineer: Professional
Consulting Engineers. General Contractor:
Howard S. Wright Construction. Lighting Designer:
Renfro Design Group

**Washington Square Village
Faculty Housing**
Apartment conversions and renovations
New York, New York
2003–4
Client: New York University

Burton Snowboards Burlington
Flagship retail store
Burlington, Vermont
2003
Client: Burton Snowboards. Architect of Record and
General Contractor: Bread Loaf

Housing Redevelopment Scheme
Conceptual design for medium-density housing,
educational spaces, and community-based
office spaces in a former industrial site
Forest Hills, New York
2003
Client: Forest City Ratner Companies

21c Museum Hotel
91-room hotel, restaurant, and
contemporary art museum
Louisville, Kentucky
2002–6
Client: Steve Wilson and Laura Lee Brown. Executive
Architect: K. Norman Berry Associates Architects.
Structural Engineer: Stanley D. Lindsey and
Associates. MEP Engineer: Kerr-Greulich Engineers.
General Contractor: James N. Gray Company.
Lighting Designer: Renfro Design Group. Graphic
Designer: Pentagram

**Serkin Center for the Performing Arts,
Marlboro College**
Concert hall, dance studio, and music and
dance classroom facility
Marlboro, Vermont
2002–5
Client: Marlboro College. Structural Engineer:
Ross Dalland PE. MEP Engineer: WV Engineering
Associates. Civil Engineer: Clough, Harbour &
Associates. Acoustical Engineer: Jaffe Holden
Acoustics. Construction Manager/Contractor: Ingram
Construction. Lighting Designer: Renfro Design Group

Upper Cross Road House
Single-family residence interior design
Greenwich, Connecticut
2002–5

Box Studios
Digital photographic enhancement facility
New York, New York
2002–4
Client: Box Studios. Structural Engineer: Ross
Dalland PE. MEP Engineer: Stanislav Slutsky PE.
Façade Consultant: Donald Baerman. General
Contractor: Taconic Builders. Code Consultant:
J. Callahan Consulting

Perdido Bay House
Single-family residence
Ono Island, Alabama
2002–4
Structural Engineer: Structural Engineering Services.
General Contractor: Blume Construction

Crosby Street Loft No. 1
Renovation and interior design
New York, New York
2002–3
General Contractor: ZZZ Carpentry

East 75th Street Penthouse
Renovation and interior design
New York, New York
2002–3
Landscape Architect: J. Mendoza Gardens. Structural
Engineer: Ross Dalland PE. MEP Engineer: Tri-Power
Engineering. General Contractor: ZZZ Carpentry

Whippoorwill Road House
Single-family residence renovation
Chappaqua, New York
2002–3
General Contractor: Brenner Builders

Corsica Drive House
Single-family residence renovation and interior
design
Pacific Palisades, California
2001–present
Landscape Architect: Blasen Landscape Architecture.
General Contractor: Charles Kuipers Design

Garden Road House
Single-family residence interior design
Scarsdale, New York
2001–5

Crestview Lane House
Single-family residence
Sagaponack, New York
2001–4
Structural Engineer: Ross Dalland PE. Mechanical
Engineer: Becht Engineering. General Contractor:
Men At Work Construction. Lighting Designer:
Renfro Design Group

Sospiro Canal House
Single-family residence and interior design
Fort Lauderdale, Florida
2001–4
Landscape Architect: Patrea Saint John. Structural
Engineer: Duckett Engineering Group. MEP Engineer:
Kamm Consulting. Civil Engineer: Flynn Engineering.
General Contractor: W. A. Bentz. Lighting Designer:
Renfro Design Group

Shelter Island House No. 1
Single-family residence
Shelter Island, New York
2001–3
General Contractor: Olinkiewicz Contracting

**Tyler School of Art, Temple University
Master Plan**
Concept design and programming for
art school relocation
Philadelphia, Pennsylvania
2001–3
Client: Temple University. MEP Engineer:
Ambrosino, DePinto & Schmieder. Civil Engineers:
Langan Engineering

Bartos Studio
Photographer's studio
New York, New York
2001–2
Client: Adam Bartos. MEP Engineer: Becht
Engineering. General Contractor: ZZZ Carpentry

East 10th Street Apartment
Renovation and interior design
New York, New York
2001–2
General Contractor: Harder Construction

Plane Space Gallery
Art gallery
New York, New York
2001–2
Client: Bryson Brodie and Chad MacDermid.
Structural Engineer: Ross Dalland PE. MEP Engineer:
Becht Engineering. General Contractor: City
Landmark Corporation. Lighting Designer: CRI.
Code Consultant: J. Callahan Consulting

West 21st Street Townhouse
Renovation
New York, New York
2001–2
Structural Engineer: Ross Dalland PE. MEP
Engineer: Becht Engineering. General Contractor:
Horizon Construction

Givenchy Perfume
Product installation
Cannes, France
2001
Client: Twist Productions

West 12th Street Loft
Renovation and interior design
New York, New York
2001
General Contractor: ZZZ Carpentry

Elberon Avenue House
Single-family residence
Loch Arbour, New Jersey
2000–2001 (unbuilt)

Elizabeth Eakins Inc
Yarn-dyeing and rug-weaving studio
and warehouse
South Norwalk, Connecticut
2000–2001
Client: Elizabeth Eakins Inc. Landscape Architect:
Christoper Kusske Landscape. Structural Engineer:
DeStefano Associates. MEP Engineer: Peter Szilagyi
Consulting Engineers. General Contractor: Lee's
Home Improvement

Fifth Avenue Apartment
Renovation
New York, New York
2000–2001
MEP Engineer: Stanislav Slutsky PE. General
Contractor: ZZZ Carpentry. Code Consultant:
J. Callahan Consulting

Gin Lane House
Single-family residence renovation
Southampton, New York
2000–2001
Structural Engineer: S. L. Maresca Consulting
Engineers. General Contractor: Andrew Hurley
Construction

Houses at Sagaponac
Single-family residence
Sagaponack, New York
2000–2001 (unbuilt)
Client: The Brown Companies

Robin Hood Foundation PS 46 Library
Elementary school library
New York, New York
2000–2001
Client: Robin Hood Foundation, New York City Board
of Education. General Contractor: Volmar Contracting.
Construction Manager: Sciame Construction

Roni Horn Studio
Artist's studio
New York, New York
2000–2001
Client: Roni Horn. General Contractor: City Landmark

Sarah's Path House
Single-family residence
Amagansett, New York
2000–2001
Structural Engineer: Ross Dalland PE. General
Contractor: Brian Mannix Builder

Tory Hill House
Single-family residence
Hillsdale, New York
2000 (unbuilt)
Landscape Architect: Margie Ruddick. Structural
Engineer: Robert Silman Associates. MEP Engineer:
Altieri Sebor Wieber. Lighting Designer: CRI

Squibnocket Pond Compound
Single-family residence and outbuildings
Aquinnah, Massachusetts
1999–2001, 2004–5
Structural Engineer: Sourati Engineering Group.
Civil Engineer: Schofield Barbini & Hoehn

Beach Street Loft
Renovation
New York, New York
1999–2001
MEP Engineer: Stanislav Slutsky PE. General
Contractor: Maverick Builders

El Dorado Apartment No. 2
Renovation and interior design
New York, New York
1999–2001
Mechanical Engineer: Stanislav Slutsky PE. General
Contractor: ZZZ Carpentry

Gardiner's Bay House No. 1
Single-family residence
Amagansett, New York
1999–2001 (unbuilt)
Structural and MEP Engineer: Ove Arup & Partners
Consulting Engineers

**Museum for African Art and Edison
Schools Headquarters**
Invited competition
New York, New York
1999–2000
Client: Edison Schools

Rogers & Goffigon Showroom
Fabric showroom
New York, New York
1999–2000
Client: Rogers & Goffigon. General Contractor:
Phoenix Construction

**Institut International de la Marionnette
Master Plan**
Analysis and expansion plan
Charleville-Mézierès, France
1999
Client: Institut International de la Marionnette

Palisades Avenue Apartment
Renovation
Fort Lee, New Jersey
1999

Wilshire Boulevard Apartment
Renovation and interior design
Pacific Palisades, California
1999

East 92nd Street Townhouse
Renovation and interior design
New York, New York
1998–2006
Structural Engineer: Ross Dalland PE. MEP
Engineer: Becht Engineering. General Contractor:
H & R Construction. Lighting Designer: Renfro
Design Group

Rogers & Goffigon
Warehouse and office renovation
Greenwich, Connecticut
1998–99, 2002–3
Client: Rogers & Goffigon. Structural Engineer: Ross
Dalland PE. General Contractor: Kriskey Carpentry

Darby Lane House
Single-family residence
East Hampton, New York
1998–2000
Landscape Architect: Margie Ruddick. Structural
Engineer: Ross Dalland PE. General Contractor:
Wright & Co. Construction

Flag Swamp Road House
Single-family residence
Roxbury, Connecticut
1998–2000
Structural Engineer: Ross Dalland PE. General
Contractor: John T. Maloney Builders

Rabbit Hill Road Compound
Single-family residence and outbuildings
Warren, Connecticut
1998–2000
Landscape Architect: Margie Ruddick. Structural
Engineer: Ross Dalland PE. General Contractor:
Picton Brothers General Contracting

East 89th Street Apartment
Renovation
New York, New York
1998–99
General Contractor: Bauhaus Construction. Code
Consultant: Agouti Construction Consulting

Mercer Street Loft No. 2
Renovation
New York, New York
1998–99
MEP Engineer: M. LaPenna Refrigeration. General
Contractor: The I. Grace Company. Interior Design:
Aero Studios. Lighting Designer: SM Lighting Design

The American Century II
Invited competition for exhibition design
New York, New York
1998
Client: Whitney Museum of American Art, New York

East 10th Street Apartment
Renovation
New York, New York
1997, 2001, 2003
MEP Engineer: Ambrosino, DePinto & Schmieder.
General Contractor: ABR Construction. Interior
Design: Todd W. Black. Code Consultant: Agouti
Construction Consulting

Marlboro College Master Plan
Plan for long-range future development for
a liberal arts college
Marlboro, Vermont
1997–2001
Client: Marlboro College. Landscape Architect:
Margie Ruddick. Civil Engineer: Peter R. Boemig.
Planning: Saucier & Flynn. Environmental
Consultant: Energysmiths

El Dorado Apartment No. 1
Renovation and interior design
New York, New York
1997–2000
MEP Engineer: Laszlo Bodak Engineer; P. A. Collins.
Sustainable Design Consultants: Green October;
Asher Derman; Steven Winter Associates; Chris
Benedict. Acoustical Engineer: Acoustic Dimensions.
General Contractor: Barzel Construction. Code
Consultant: J. Callahan Consulting

Yale School of Art and New Theater
Adaptive reuse and new construction for
art school and theater
New Haven, Connecticut
1997–2000
Client: Yale University. Structural Engineer: Robert
Silman Associates. MEP Engineer: Flack + Kurtz. Civil
Engineer: URS Greiner. Construction Manager: Dimeo
Construction Company. Theater Consultant: Fisher
Dachs Associates. Lighting Designer: Gary Gordon

Central Park West Apartment No. 2
Renovation and interior design
New York, New York
1997–99
General Contractor: Maverick Builders. Lighting
Designer: Gary Gordon. Code Consultant: Agouti
Construction Consulting

East 72nd Street Townhouse
Townhouse renovation and artist's studio
New York, New York
1997–99
Landscape Architect: Margie Ruddick. Consulting
Engineer: Stanislav Slutsky PE. Structural Engineer:
Ross Dalland PE. Mechanical Engineer: Ambrosino,
DePinto & Schmieder. General Contractor: ZZZ
Carpentry. Interior Design: Bruce Bierman Design.
Lighting Designer: Gary Gordon. Code Consultant:
Agouti Construction Consulting

Woodside Avenue House
Single-family residence renovation and addition
Westport, Connecticut
1997–99
Landscape Architect: Christoper Kusske Landscape.
Structural Engineer: Ross Dalland PE. General
Contractor: Lee's Home Improvement

Stable Way Compound
Single-family residence and outbuildings
Cornwall-on-Hudson, New York
1997–98
Landscape Architect: Margie Ruddick. Structural
Engineer: Ross Dalland PE

West 11th Street Apartment
Renovation
New York, New York
1997–98
Code Consultant: Agouti Construction Consulting

The Center for Photography at Woodstock
Master plan funded by New York State Council
on the Arts
Woodstock, New York
1997
Client: The Center for Photography at Woodstock.
Consulting Engineer: North Engineers &
Design Associates

Cynthia Steffe
Women's boutique in Bloomingdale's
New York, New York
1997
Client: Cynthia Steffe

Perry Street Loft No. 2
Renovation
New York, New York
1997
General Contractor: ABR Construction

Perry Street Loft No. 1
Renovation
New York, New York
1997
General Contractor: Sweeney Construction. Code
Consultant: Agouti Construction Consulting

Club Monaco
Store design concept and rollout
Boston, Chicago, Los Angeles, Miami,
New York (Midtown), New York (SoHo),
Pasadena (unbuilt), San Francisco (unbuilt),
Washington, D.C.
1996–2000
Client: Club Monaco International. Architect of
Record: Nadel Architects (California). Structural
Engineer: Robert Silman Associates (New York).
MEP Engineer: Ambrosino, DePinto & Schmieder
(New York). Lighting Designer: Chad Rains

Mercer Street Loft No. 1
Renovation
New York, New York
1996–98
General Contractor: The Pros From Dover. Code
Consultant: Agouti Construction Consulting

Barrow Street Apartment
Renovation
New York, New York
1996–97
Structural Engineer: Ross Dalland PE. General
Contractor: Harder Construction

Howell Studio
Artist's studio and loft
New York, New York
1996–97
Mechanical Engineer: Rana and Guth Engineers.
General Contractor: ZZZ Carpentry. Code
Consultant: Agouti Construction Consulting

Prince Street Loft
Renovation
New York, New York
1996–97
Consulting Engineer: John J. Guth Associates.
Code Consultant: Agouti Construction Consulting

Duane Street Loft
Artist's studio and loft
New York, New York
1996
General Contractor: Westin Construction. Code
Consultant: Agouti Construction Consulting

cK Calvin Klein
Store design concept and rollout
Hong Kong, Jakarta, London, Milan, New York,
Rome, Singapore
1995–99
Client: Calvin Klein Inc. Collaborators: Stefano Carmi
Architetto (Milan)

Cerulean Estate
Eight-room luxury oceanfront inn
Anguilla, British West Indies
1995–97
Client: Cerulean Ltd. Consulting Engineer: Nowell
Warren Rogers. MEP Engineer: Ambrosino, DePinto
& Schmieder. General Contractor: Anguilla Post and
Beam. Interior Design: Warren Sutton Design

Johnson Hill House
Single-family residence renovation and addition
Chester, Massachusetts
1995–97 (unbuilt)
Structural Engineer: Ross Dalland PE

Riverside Drive Apartment
Renovation
New York, New York
1995–96
General Contractor: ZZZ Carpentry

Shinnecock Bay House
Single-family residence renovation
Hampton Bays, New York
1995–96
General Contractor: S.G.C. Construction

Dorset Hill House
Single-family residence renovation and addition
Dorset, Vermont
1995

Narrow Lane House
Single-family residence renovation and addition
Bridgehampton, New York
1995

Wegman Studio
Renovation
New York, New York
1995
Client: William Wegman. Structural Engineer: Anchor
Consulting. MEP Engineer: Stanislav Slutsky PE.
General Contractor: ZZZ Carpentry. Code Consultant:
J. Callahan Consulting

West 18th Street Loft
Renovation
New York, New York
1995
Structural Engineer: Anchor Consulting. MEP
Engineer: Stanislav Slutsky PE. General Contractor:
ZZZ Carpentry. Code Consultant: J. Callahan
Consulting

Hope Branch Library
Community library
Hope, Indiana
1994–98
Client: Bartholomew County Public Library; Cummins
Engine Foundation. Architect of Record: Veazey
Parrott & Shoulders. Structural Engineer: Robert
Silman Associates. MEP Engineer: Veazey Parrott &
Shoulders. General Contractor: Repp & Mundt

Sagaponack Road House
Single-family residence renovation and addition
Sagaponack, New York
1994–97
Structural Engineer: Ross Dalland PE. General
Contractor: Wright and Co. Construction

Battery Park City Parks Conservancy
Headquarters for parks management,
recreation and programming, and
maintenance organization
New York, New York
1994–96
Client: Battery Park City Authority. Structural
Enigineer: Robert Silman Associates. MEP Engineer:
Atkinson Koven Feinberg Engineers. Acoustical
Engineer: Jaffe Holden Scarbrough Acoustics. Code
Consultant: Agouti Construction Consulting

Oak Trail Road House
Single-family residence renovation
Englewood, New Jersey
1994–96

Central Park West Apartment No. 1
Renovation and interior design
New York, New York
1993–95
Interior Design: Rice & Clark Interior Design

Conyers Farm House
Single-family residence
North Castle, New York
1993–95
General Contractor: Bourke & Matthews

Bay State Road Barn
Single-family residence renovation
Rehoboth, Massachusetts
1993–94
Structural Engineer: Ross Dalland PE

Douglaston Parkway House
Single-family residence renovation and addition
Douglaston, New York
1993–94
General Contractor: Eamon Burke

Duck Pond House
Single-family residence
Louisville, Kentucky
1993–94
Structural Engineer: Ross Dalland PE. General
Contractor: Glenn Coxon Builders

Lake House
Single-family residence
Red Lake, Minnesota
1993–94

Red Creek Pond House
Single-family residence addition
Hampton Bays, New York
1993–94

West 15th Street Loft
Renovation
New York, New York
1993–94
General Contractor: Westin Construction. Code
Consultant: Agouti Construction Consulting

West Ruskin Street House
Single-family residence
Seaside, Florida
1993
Architect: Berke & McWhorter Architects

Kenilworth Apartment
Renovation
New York, New York
1992, 1997–99
General Contractor: ZZZ Carpentry

Baron & Baron Inc.
Graphic and product design studio and offices
New York, New York
1992–93, 1998
Client: Baron & Baron Inc. General Contractor:
Westin Construction

Alameda Naval Air Station
Adaptive reuse proposal solicited by
Progressive Architecture magazine
Alameda, California
1992
Client: *Progressive Architecture* magazine

Zoglio Homes
Modular homes designed as part of
a citywide housing revitalization effort
Providence, Rhode Island
1992 (unbuilt)
Client: David Zoglio, Plantation Homes

East Ruskin Street Townhouse
Single-family residence
Seaside, Florida
1991–92 (unbuilt)
Architect: Berke & McWhorter Architects

The Stephen Talkhouse
Renovation and addition to live music venue
Amagansett, New York
1990–94
Client: Peter Honerkamp, Tim Meyers, Loren Gallo, and Kevin Finnegan. Structural Engineer: Ross Dalland PE. General Contractor: David Virgil Architect Design/Build

White Street Loft
Renovation
New York, New York
1990–92
Structural Engineer: Ross Dalland PE. General Contractor: Westin Construction. Code Consultant: Agouti Construction Consulting

Industria Superstudio
Adaptive reuse of automotive garage into fashion photography studio and restaurant
New York, New York
1990–91
Client: Industria Superstudio. Structural Engineer: Ross Dalland PE. Mechanical Contractor: M. LaPenna Refrigeration. Electrical Engineer: I. P. Group. General Contractor: G. P. Winter Associates. Lighting Designer: Lalomia Lighting. Code Consultant: Agouti Construction Consulting

Windham Hill House
Single-family residence renovation and addition
Windham, Vermont
1990–91
Structural Engineer: Ross Dalland PE. Civil Engineer: Criterium Lalancette Engineers. General Contractor: Stephen W. Thurston Builder

Abingdon Square Penthouse
Renovation
New York, New York
1989, 1992, 1994, 2005–7
Structural Engineer: Ross Dalland PE. General Contractor: ZZZ Carpentry. Code Consultant: Agouti Construction Consulting

Halley Studio
Artist's studio
North Hillsdale, New York
1989–92
Client: Peter Halley. Architect: Berke & McWhorter Architects

The New American Home
Model home for *Builder* magazine for the National Association of Homebuilders Annual Convention
Atlanta, Georgia
1989–90
Client: *Builder* magazine

Pensacola Street House
Single-family residence
Seaside, Florida
1989–90

East Ruskin Street House No. 4
Single-family residence
Seaside, Florida
1989

West 9th Street Apartment
Renovation
New York, New York
1989
General Contractor: ZZZ Carpentry. Code Consultant: Agouti Construction Consulting

Modica Market
Grocery store and community meeting hall
Seaside, Florida
1988, 1991
Client: Charles and Sarah Modica. Architect of Record: Destin Architectural Group. Acoustical Engineer: Jaffe Acoustics

Moosepac Residential Master Plan
210-unit master plan for single-family housing development
Jefferson Township, New Jersey
1988–89
Client: Gerber Development. Civil Engineer: Beardslee Engineering Associates

North Wood Commons
4 modular house designs
Haverhill, Massachusetts
1988–89 (unbuilt)
Client: Essex Associates

Hamilton College Campus Landscape
Invited competition to design pathways and outdoor space
Clinton, New York
1988
Client: Hamilton College

The Library Power Project
Renovations of 150 New York City public school libraries
New York, New York
1987–95
Client: American Reading Council and Fund for New York City Public Education

Forest Street House
Single-family residence
Seagrove Beach, Florida
1987–89

Gerber Modular Houses
Designs of 12 modular houses at economy, moderate, and luxury price ranges
1987–89
Client: Museum Development Corp.

Northwest Hill Road House
Renovation of one-room schoolhouse into
single-family residence
Williamstown, Massachusetts
1987–88
Consulting Engineer: Warren M. Lowry. General
Contractor: Bump & McAlpine Builders

East Ruskin Street House No. 3
Single-family residence
Seaside, Florida
1987

East Ruskin Street House No. 2
Single-family residence
Seaside, Florida
1987
General Contractor: Warnerworks

**North Cove Yacht Harbor,
Battery Park City**
Yacht marina
New York, New York
1987
Client: South Cove Associates/Watermark Associates.
Owner: BPCA. Developer: Watermark Associates.
Executive Architect: Carl Meinhardt. Structural
Engineer: Meuser Rutledge Consulting Engineers.
MEP Engineer: DLB Associates. Construction
Manager: Kreisler Borg Florman General Construction

Savannah Street House No. 6
Single-family residence
Seaside, Florida
1987
General Contractor: Warnerworks

Savannah Street House No. 5
Single-family residence
Seaside, Florida
1987

Per-spi-cas-ity
Open-air beachfront market
Seaside, Florida
1986, 1991–93
Client: Daryl Davis and Mary Patton

Brooklyn Port Authority Piers Master Plan
Master plan for Brooklyn Piers 1–5
Brooklyn, New York
1986–87 (unbuilt)
Client: Watermark Associates. Executive Architect:
Carl Meinhardt

White River House
Single-family residence
Indianapolis, Indiana
1986–87
General Contractor: E. B. Rayburn Construction

Hoboken Houses
Façades for infill rowhouses
Hoboken, New Jersey
1986
Client: Museum Development Corp. Architect of
Record: Tom Cusanelli. Consulting Engineer:
Andrew J. Desiderio

Savannah Street House No. 3
Single-family residence
Seaside, Florida
1986

Savannah Street House No. 2
Single-family residence
Seaside, Florida
1985–86
General Contractor: New Creation Homes

Apple Lane House
Single-family residence
Point Washington, Florida
1985

**Snow Chapel, Church of the Holy
Archangels**
Private Russian Orthodox chapel
Star Tannery, Virginia
1985 (unbuilt)

Savannah Street House No. 1
Single-family residence
Seaside, Florida
1984

Tupelo Street House No. 2
Single-family residence
Seaside, Florida
1984
General Contractor: Warnerworks

Tupelo Street Tower
Single-family residence
Seaside, Florida
1983, 1987

Tupelo Street House No. 1
Single-family residence
Seaside, Florida
1983
General Contractor: Warnerworks

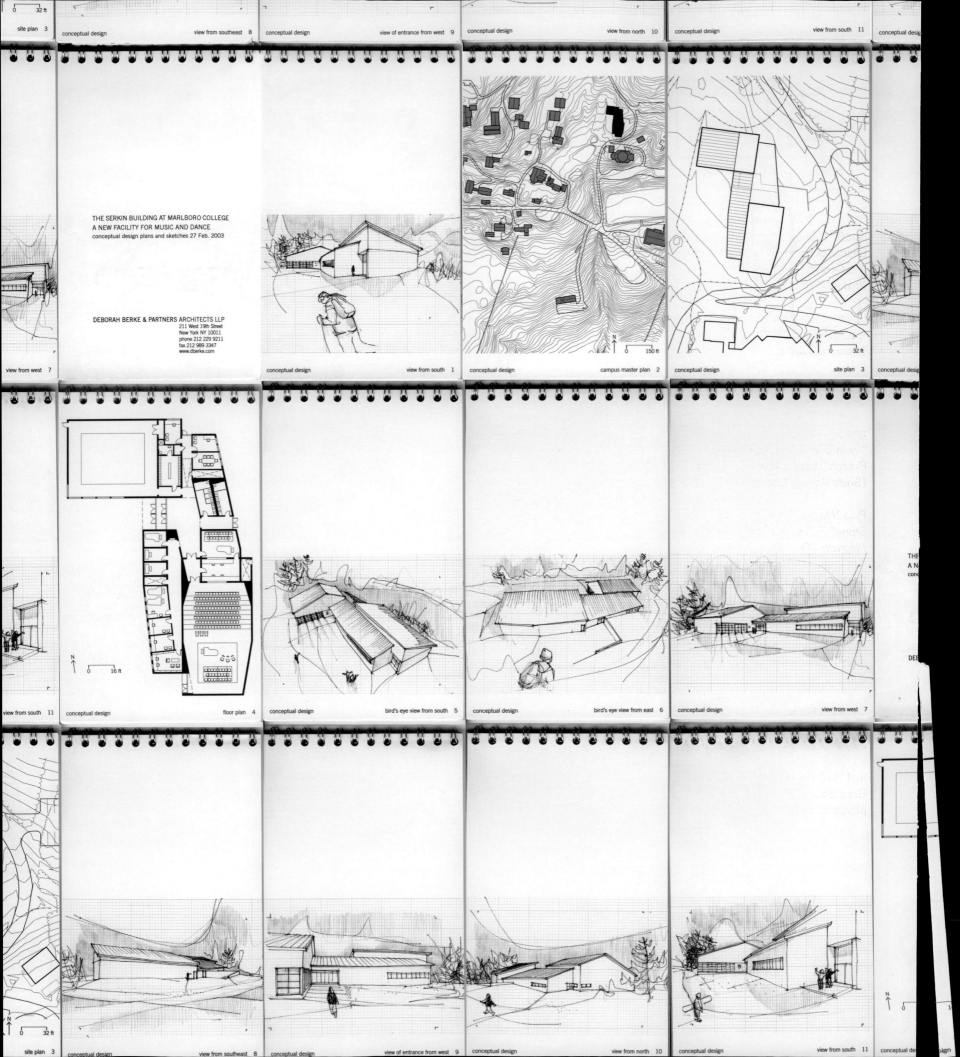

Selected Bibliography

2008

Editors of Phaidon Press, *Atlas of 21st Century Architecture*, London: Phaidon Press

Editors of Verlagshaus Braun, *1000 x Architecture of the Americas*, Berlin: Verlagshaus Braun

Sabina Marreiros, ed., *Art Hotels*, Singapore: Page One Group

2007

"Irwin Union Bank, Creekview Branch," *Interior World Magazine* (South Korea), December, 148–53

Pilar Viladas, "Living over the Store," *T: The New York Times Style Magazine*, October 7, 154–59

Dominic Bradbury, "Long Island House," *Homes & Gardens*, October, 149–53

Alan G. Brake, "Lone Star Berke," *The Architect's Newspaper*, July 4, 1, 6

Cathleen McGuigan, "A Certain Sense of Calm," *Newsweek*, July 2–9, 52–64

Jeff VanDam, "Female Bonding on Bond Street," *New York Times*, March 4

Hilary Lewis, "The New Florida Home No. 1: House and a Half," *HOME Fort Lauderdale* and *HOME Miami*, January, 25–29

Bradley Lincoln, "On Ontario: Deborah Berke Blows into the Windy City with the Chic James Hotel," *Interior Design*, January, 208–14

2006

Jen DeRose, "Best of Year: Hotel," *Interior Design*, December, 50–51

Anna Margrét Björnsson, "Fágen í hversdagsleikanum" ("Everyday Elegance"), *Fréttablaðið* (Iceland), October 14, 2

Dominic Bradbury, "Private View," *Condé Nast Traveller* (U.K. ed.), October, 82

Lloyd Jackson, "The Florida Room: An Exercise in Extraordinary Furniture Design," *HOME Miami*, October, 42–45

Kristi Cameron, "Glamming It Up," *Metropolis*, September, 33–34

Susan O'Keefe and Amy Alipio, "Hotel Confidential," *National Geographic Traveler*, September

Alan G. Brake, "By the Beautiful C," *pitch: Kentucky Arts & Culture*, pre-fall, 16–20

Eva Hagberg, "Best in the Midwest," *Wallpaper**, August, 156–62

John King, "Columbus Explored," *Dwell*, July/August, 170–82

Julie Sinclair Eakin, "Borrowers and Lenders: The Newest Bank in Columbus, Indiana, Looks Forward and Back Simultaneously," *Architecture*, July, 14–15

Jenny Comita, "Louisville Sluggers," *W*, July, 106–13

Leigh Anne Miller, "Art Checks into Kentucky," *Art in America*, June/July, 51

William Weathersby, Jr., "21c Museum Hotel: Art and Commerce Meet in This Hybrid Building Type," *Architectural Record*, June, 304–8

"21c Museum Hotel," *Interior World Magazine* (South Korea), June, 156–63

Raul Barreneche, "Viewing Rooms," *TRAVEL + LEISURE*, June, 262–68

Rebecca Goldberg, "James Does Chicago: Deborah Berke Styles the James Hotel for Business," *Boutique Design*, summer, 24–25

Paul L. Underwood, "Louisville Weekend," *New York Times Magazine*, summer, 38

Diane Heilenman, "Mr. and Mrs. Modern Art," *Courier-Journal* (Louisville), March 28

Chris Poynter, "Arty, Modern 21c Offers Feast for the Senses," *Courier-Journal* (Louisville), March 28

Paul L. Underwood, "The Art Hotel," *New York Times*, March 19

2005

Elaine Greene, "Extraordinary," *Metropolitan Home*, November, 140–45

Lloyd Jackson, "Living with Art," *HOME Fort Lauderdale*, September, 67–74

Pilar Viladas, "Florida Rooms: A House Where Light, Views and Art Coexist under One Roof," *New York Times Magazine*, June 19, 48–53

Esther da Costa Meyer and Anne T. Makeever, "Women in Architecture: The Pioneers Who Rewrote the Rules and Intimate One-on-Ones with Those Making History Now," *To the Trade*, spring, 86–87

2004
Ingrid Whitehead, "James Hotel,"
Architectural Record, August, 144–47

Gisela Williams, "Praising Arizona,"
Wallpaper*, July/August, 172–73

Mitchell Owens, "Hot Property,"
TRAVEL + LEISURE, July, 134–41

Katherine Harris, "Sizzling in
Scottsdale," *Interior Design,*
June, 194–200

Elaine Louie, "Color Palette
Courtesy of Desert," *New York
Times,* February 5

2003
Coco Brown, ed., *American Dream:
The Houses at Sagaponac—Modern
Living in the Hamptons,* essays by
Richard Meier and Alastair Gordon,
New York: Rizzoli, 48–51

Cathleen McGuigan, "The
McMansion Next Door: Why the
American House Needs a
Makeover," *Newsweek,* October 27,
85–86

Raul Barreneche, "Loft in Space,"
Metropolitan Home, September/
October, 152–59

Jane Margolies, "A Glorious
Tapestry," *Interior Design,*
June, 176–83

Zoe Ryan, "Behind the Scenes,"
CITY, May/June, 50–53

"Everyday Architect," *Index,*
February/March, 26

2002
Jen Renzi, "Hall of Fame 2002:
Deborah Berke," *Interior Design,*
December, S18–21

Meghan Drueding, "Home Front,"
Residential Architect, July, 22–23

Alexa Yablonski, ed.,
"Everyday Elegance," *Interior
Design,* May, 130

Jessica Dheere, ed., "What Should
Lower Manhattan Look Like?" *Art
News,* April, 125

2001
"Interior Architecture Awards:
Deborah Berke, Architect, Art
Director's Loft, Manhattan," *Oculus,*
December, 36

Matt Tyrnauer, "Der Mann,
Der Alles Kann," *Architectural
Digest* (German ed.), August/
September, 20–24

K. Michael Hays, Julie Iovine, and
Gwendolyn Wright, "Exceptionally
Ordinary," *Architecture,* June, 90–101

Susan Kleinman, "A+ for Aardvark,"
Metropolitan Home, May/June,
140–49

Matt Tyrnauer, "Baron by Design,"
Vanity Fair, May, 176–83, 212–13

Gavin Hogben, "New Art Building
for Yale," *Yale Constructs,* spring, 15

Julie Iovine, "A-List Alternative to
Hamptons Hulk," *New York Times,*
March 8

Martin Filler, "Deborah Berke,"
House Beautiful, March, 48–52

2000
Cheryl Weber, "Simply Perfect,"
Residential Architect, August, 42–49

1999
Anna Muoio and Lucy A. McCauley,
eds., "Unit of One: Design Rules,"
Fast Company, October, 130

Holly Brubach, "The 25 Smartest
Women in America," *Mirabella,*
September, 119

Francesca Benvenuti, "In Punta di
Design," *Spazio Casa,* May, 84–91

Gavin Hogben, "Architecture of
the Everyday," *Yale Constructs,*
spring, 14

1998
Wendy Goodman, "The Stark
Report," *New York Magazine,*
October 1, 50–53

Joseph Giovannini, "Light of Hand:
A New York Loft Proves Less Is
Definitely More," *Metropolitan
Home* (U.K. ed.), September/
October, 150–55

Henry Urbach, "Everyday Sublime,"
Interior Design, September, 186–95

Abby Bussel, "Free Plan," *Interior
Design,* April, 224–27

Akiko Busch, "By Design,"
Metropolis, April, 53–58

Eleanor Charles, "For Connecticut,
Home-Grown Modulars," *New York
Times,* January 31

"Deborah Berke with Peter Halley,"
Index, January/February, 30–37

1997
Steven Harris and Deborah Berke,
eds., *Architecture of the
Everyday,* New York: Princeton
Architectural Press

Henry Urbach, "Basic Instincts,"
Interior Design, September, 156–59

Jayne Merkel, "Apartments
and Lofts: The New Humility,"
Oculus, June

Jane Withers, "Fashion's Empire
Builders," *Harper's Bazaar,*
March, 344–49

Pamela J. Wilson, "Indiana Enlightenment," *Traditional Home,* March, 100–111

Jane Withers, "The New Minimalism," *Oculus*, January

1996
Steven Brooke, *Seaside*, Gretna, La.: Pelican Publishing, passim

Julie Iovine, "Minimalism," *New York Times,* September 26

Tyler Brûlé, "The Making of Miss Minimalism," *Wallpaper**, September/October, 19–21

Alexandra Lange, "Chic Simple," *New York Magazine: Design 1996*, March 25, 55, 70–77

1995
Brian Blair, "Hope Branch Library Design Captures 'Feel' of Town," *The Republic*, May 19, A1

1993
Julie Iovine, "A Working House," *Architectural Record,* April, 90–93

Charles Gandee, "Leaving Her Blueprint," *Vogue*, April, 384–88, 464

1992
Michael Gross, "Inside Industria Superstudio: The Style Factory," *New York Magazine*, November 16, 46–55

Kevin Cobb, "New York's Star Studio," *American Photo*, September/October, 50–53

James Servin, "Studio! Lifestyle! Empire?" *New York Times*, April 16

Jane Margolies, "Halfway to Paradise," *House Beautiful,* April, 96–103

1991
David Mohney and Keller Easterling, eds., *Seaside: Making a Town in America*, New York: Princeton Architectural Press, 118–33

Phil Patton, "In Seaside, Florida, the Forward Thing Is to Look Backward," *Smithsonian*, January, 85–86, 90

1990
"Women in American Architecture," *Space Design: Special Issue: Women in American Architecture*, June, 48–49

1989
Beth Dunlop, "Coming of Age," *Architectural Record*, July, 96–103

Martin Filler, "Seaside Village," *Ambiente* (Germany), June, 150–60

———, "Model Houses," *House & Garden*, April, 44

"Vernacular," *Architectural Review*, February, 80–85

1988
Joan Ockman, Deborah Berke, Mary McLeod, and Beatriz Colomina, eds., *Architectureproduction*, New York: Princeton Architectural Press

Clifford Pearson, ed., "Builder's Choice Merit Award—Sward Cottage," *Builder,* October, 171

Philip Langdon, "A Good Place to Live," *Atlantic Monthly,* March, 44–45

1987
"Die Ferienstadt Seaside in Florida," *Baumeister* (Germany), September, 64–65

1986
Andrew MacNair, "Forty under Forty," *Interiors*, September, 161

Susan Zevon, "Small-Town America by the Sea," *House Beautiful*, January, 78–85

1985
Joan Ockman, ed., *Architecture Criticism Ideology*, Princeton: Princeton Architectural Press

Acknowledgments

It took the assistance and support of many people to make this book, and many more to make the projects documented within it. To everyone I have worked for and with over the years, thank you.

In my office, I am ever grateful for the hugely creative efforts of the four senior people in the firm: Stephen Brockman and Caroline Wharton, and my partners, Maitland Jones and Marc Leff. It would take many pages to name every employee and collaborator, contractor and consultant, whose efforts contributed to the success of the work, but Catherine Bird, Robert Schultz, and Carey McWhorter deserve special mention.

I want to acknowledge all of my clients for their faith in our vision; I have learned much from your engagement in our process. Certain individual clients not only believed in the philosophy behind the architecture but also contributed to shaping the architecture itself: Will Miller, Edwin Schlossberg, Marianne Boesky, David Horvitz and Francie Bishop-Good, Steve Wilson and Laura Lee Brown, and Teri and Barry Volpert. Your responses from across the table improved the results.

I have been very fortunate to have received the support and criticism of trusted friends, including Joan Ockman, Mary McLeod, Cathleen McGuigan, and Meg Fidler. I would also like to extend a special thanks to Amy Hempel for her exquisitely taut foreword. To them, and to all my dear friends who were with me through this process, I have appreciated your insights.

To my students at Yale over the many years, thank you for your willingness to trust in my unusual project programs and for your provocative work in response. I am indebted to all of you, as well as to my valued colleagues, in particular, Steven Harris and Alec Purves.

The book itself could not have been realized without the efforts of Tracy Myers, Diana Murphy, and Miko McGinty, and I am grateful for their hard work and determination to see it published. I would also like to thank Michelle Komie, our liaison at Yale University Press, as well as the photographers whose images are featured in the book, in particular, Victoria Sambunaris and Catherine Tighe.

Finally, none of this would have been possible without the unconditional support of my family. This book is dedicated to my daughter, Tess; my husband, Peter; my mother, Beverly; and to the memory of my father, Robert. He launched my aspirations.

Deborah Berke

The opportunity to immerse oneself in the study of an architect's body of work—to contemplate its qualities, both manifest and more elusive; savor the pleasure of experiencing it; and slowly earn the satisfaction of truly understanding it—is an unusual luxury. Equally rare is the chance to work with a person of Deborah Berke's great intelligence, straightforwardness, and integrity, and I am deeply honored to have been entrusted with interpreting her work. Doing justice to that work is a large responsibility, and it is only with the assistance and support of numerous people that I have been able to meet it.

My comprehension of Deborah's oeuvre was vastly enriched by the many site visits that were so kindly facilitated by her clients; their generosity to me and their affection for Deborah speak volumes. The firm's entire staff was unfailingly helpful and accommodating, and careful, insightful readings of the text by Deborah's partners, Maitland Jones and Marc Leff, forced me to ever greater clarity.

I owe an enormous debt of gratitude to Diana Murphy for bringing me together with Deborah and graphic designer Miko McGinty, and for her singular skill and patience in pushing me to hone and perfect the words. Miko's elegant design provides a perfect graphic backdrop for what I hope are thought-provoking but straightforward arguments.

I must recognize the encouragement and wisdom of good friends and colleagues Elisabeth Agro, Donald Albrecht, Lu Donnelly, Paul Lewis, Thomas Reynolds, Joseph Rosa, and Caren Winnall. To Richard Armstrong, The Henry J. Heinz II Director of Carnegie Museum of Art, I offer my appreciation for his support of this project.

Finally, I extend my love and thanks to my father, George F. Myers. He is both my greatest cheerleader and a true model of determination and candor.

Tracy Myers

Deborah Berke & Partners Architects LLP
Deborah Berke Architect PC
Berke & McWhorter Architects
Deborah Berke Architect
1983–2008

Emily Abruzzo
William Agostinho
Damaris Arias
Deborah Berke
Andrew Berman
Noah Biklen
Catherine Bird
Benjamin Bischoff
Peter Bogaczewicz
Miche Booz
Zachary Brennan
Patricia Brett
Stephen Brockman
Chad Broussard
Emily Chaffee
Stephanie Christoff
Roberto Cipriano, Jr.
Michael Decker
Marina De Conciliis
Joeylynn Demeo
Kiki Dennis
Eli Derman
Jennifer Duhamel
Shavon Durham
Julie Eakin
Luisa Fabian
Ira Frazin
Yelenyn Garcia
Glenn Garrison
Margaret Gorman
Rachael Gray
Jeff Haines
Gregory Haley
Christopher Harnish
Melanie Hennigan

Ameet Hiremath
Sarah Holton
Aaron Hunt
Richard Irving
Jean Jaminet
Jonathan Jones
Maitland Jones
Ryan Keiper
Matthew Kelley
Rhoda Kennedy
Melanie Kim
Stephanie Lam
Stephane LeBlanc
Andrew Ledbetter
Marc Leff
Amy Lelyveld
Shirley Leong
Marissa Levin
Mario Marchant
Elizabeth McLendon
Carey McWhorter
Emily Meza
Jacquelyn Moore-Hill
Jennifer Moye
Simon Murray
Nathan Nagai
Christina Nastos
Melissa Nosal
David O'Brien
Laurence Odfjell
Miyako Panalaks
Jonathan Parisen
Nicholas Pestiau
Daniel Pontius
Stephani Resch

William Reue
Lourdes Reynafarje
Gitta Robinson
Christopher Romero
Faith Rose
Michelle Rossomando
Caroline Schiele
Terrence Schroeder
Robert Schultz
Heather Snyder
Genevieve Sopchuk
Scott Specht
Stephanie Spoto
Bradley Stephens
Courtney Stern
Alexandra Tailer
Maki Takenouchi
Megumi Tamahana
Karina Tengberg
Bronwen Thomas
Jennifer Tobias
Caleb Todd
Brandon Townsend
Kieran Trihey
J. Tom Tulloch
Simon Vargas
Joan Vasciana
Irina Verona
Jane Wechsler
Grzegorz Weglarksi
Caroline Wharton
Scott Wing
Adam Yarinsky
Christopher Yost

Photography Credits

Fabien Baron
22

Eric Boman
77

Steven Brooke
185, 188 top, 189

Deborah Berke & Partners
Architects
94, 98 left, 184

Chris Floyd
Jacket front, 41–43, 44 top, 45

Gentl & Hyers
166

Eduard Hueber/archphoto
11, 36, 97, 117, 123, 153, 162, jacket back

The James Chicago
78 left, 83, 84 top

Courtesy Beate Forberg Johansen
17

Nikolas Koenig
20–21, 144, 147

Eric Laignel
82, 84 bottom

Mark Luscombe-Whyte
60 top, 62, 63, 100

Victoria Sambunaris
30–31, 37, 65, 66, 67 bottom left
and bottom right, 68, 69, 99, 114–15,
126–29, 160–61, 164–65, 167–71,
186–87, 191, 192 bottom, 193–95,
200–201, 203–11, 217–22, 224, 228–33

Annie Schlechter
95 bottom, 103

Jason Schmidt
122 right, 254

Catherine Tighe
Frontispiece, 15, 23, 33–35, 46, 47
bottom, 48 bottom, 49, 51, 52, 54, 55,
57–59, 60 bottom, 71, 72 top, 73, 75,
76, 79, 80 top, 81, 85, 93, 96 bottom,
104–6, 109–13, 118–21, 137–39, 141–43,
145 right, 146, 148–51, 154 left, 155 right,
159, 172–73, 175–83, 213–15, 225

Paul Warchol
125, 132, 135, 158, 162, 163, 197, 198
bottom, 199

Alex Williams
92